900

D0307891

Historical Association Studies
General Editors: Roger Mettam and James Shields

Decolonization
The Fall of the European Empires
M. E. Chamberlain

Gandhi
Antony Copley

The Counter-Reformation
N. S. Davidson

British Radicalism and the French Revolution 1789–1815
H. T. Dickinson

From Luddism to the First Reform Bill
Reform in England 1810–1832
J. R. Dinwiddy

Radicalism in the English Revolution 1640–1660
F. D. Dow

The New Monarchy
England, 1471–1534
Anthony Goodman

The French Reformation
Mark Greengrass

Politics in the Reign of Charles II
K. H. D. Haley

Occupied France
Collaboration and Resistance 1940–1944
H. R. Kedward

Britain's Decline
Problems and Perspectives
Alan Sked

Bismarck
Bruce Waller

The Russian Revolution 1917–1921
Beryl Williams

The Historical Association, 59a Kennington Park Road,
London SE11 4JH

The New Monarchy

England, 1471–1534

ANTHONY GOODMAN

Basil Blackwell

First published 1988

Basil Blackwell Ltd
108 Cowley Road, Oxford, OX4 1JF, UK

Basil Blackwell Inc.
432 Park Avenue South, Suite 1503
New York, NY 10016, USA

British Library Cataloguing in Publication Data

Goodman, Anthony
   The new monarchy: England 1471–1534.
   — (Historical Association studies).
   1. Monarchy, British — History
   2. Great Britain — History — 1066–1687
   3. Great Britain — Kings and rulers
   I. Title II. Series
   354.4103′12′09   JN337

   ISBN   0–631–14927–9

Library of Congress Cataloging in Publication Data

Goodman, Anthony, 1936–
   The new monarchy: England, 1471–1534/Anthony Goodman.
      p. cm. — (Historical Association studies)
   Bibliography: p.
   Includes index.
   ISBN 0–631–14927–9 (pbk.)
   1. Great Britain—Politics and government—1485–1603. 2. Great
Britain–Politics and government—1399–1485. 3. Monarchy—Great
Britain—History. 4. Tudor, House of. 5. York, House of. 6. Kings and
rulers, Medieval. I. Title. II. Series.
DA325.G66 1988
942.05—dc19   87–35573

Typeset in 10 on 11 pt Baskerville by
Photo·Graphics, Honiton, Devon
Printed in Great Britain by Whitstable Litho Ltd., Whitstable, Kent

Contents

For my father and stepmother,
Joseph and Alice Goodman

Acknowledgements

I am grateful to Professor H. T. Dickinson for encouraging me to write this study and to Dr Virginia Murphy for her expert appraisal. Ms Alison Munro typed the script in an exemplary manner.

1 Concepts of Yorkist and Early Tudor Monarchy

Advocates of 'New Monarchy' Theories

The idea that the Yorkist and early Tudor kings created a new kind of monarchical authority was first expounded by J. R. Green in his *Short History of the English People* (1893). He entitled a chapter 'The New Monarchy, 1422–1540', but he applied the phrase specifically to the period 1471–1509. He identified the founder of this monarchy as Edward IV (reigned 1461–70, 1471–83). What Green meant by 'new monarchy' was the introduction of despotism. He argued that the liberties established by parliament since the time of Edward I (reigned 1272–1307) were extinguished as a result of the crushing of baronial power which was a consequence of the Wars of the Roses (1455–85). These liberties were 'the right of freedom from arbitrary taxation, from arbitrary legislation, from arbitrary imprisonment, and the responsibility of even the highest servants of the Crown to Parliament and to the law'.

Green asserted that 'The old English kingship, limited by the forces of feudalism or of the religious sanctions wielded by the priesthood or by the progress of constitutional freedom, faded suddenly away, and in its place we see, all-absorbing and unrestrained, the despotism of the New Monarchy.' This was promoted not only by the decline of baronial power, but by a heightening of social tensions: 'It was indeed . . . this social danger [from the populace] which lay at the root of the Tudor despotism. For the proprietary classes the repression of the poor was a question of life and death.'

Green's theory that there was a new monarchy was generally accepted. But historians tended to ignore the role of the Yorkist kings in creating it, or to treat their reigns as a prologue to its appearance. Moreover, his dark thesis that the new monarchy was an aberration in the progress of English liberty, sustained by fear of revolution, was to be modified. A. F. Pollard, biographer of Wolsey and Henry VIII, put forward a more positive interpretation which for long held sway. In a chapter on the European phenomenon of 'The New Monarchy' in *Factors in Modern History* (1910), he argued that Tudor rule essentially embodied the will of 'progressive' opinion and promoted beneficial modernizing trends which helped to create the centralized national state. Monarchy survived, profiting from the decay of other institutions in the fifteenth century, because 'it was the embodiment of the coming force of nationality.... Men were tired of politics; they wanted peace ... They cared little for parliamentary principles ... Magna Carta was buried in oblivion ... Such were the tendencies which the kings of the New Monarchy crystallised into practical weapons of absolute government.'

Pollard was to show an appreciation of the continuities between medieval and early Tudor government. He argued that the Tudor novelty was a return to a more orderly system of government, reflected in Edward I's legislation. He insisted that the 'absolutism' of the Tudors did not weaken parliament, the corner-stone of English liberties: 'we shall find that Henry VIII especially was anything but hostile to his Parliaments; that under him the Parliamentary system is extended and developed; that Parliamentary privileges are asserted and maintained; and that Parliament is educated up to a sense of national duty' (1910).

With the support of Pollard's authority the reputation of the early Tudor monarchy soared. It was seen as a decisive instrument in the development of the nation-state. Between the World Wars the study of the Tudor period intensified; notable examples were the two volumes on *Early Tudor Government* by K. Pickthorn (1934a,b). Relatively little was published on fifteenth-century institutions prior to 1485. The events of 1485 were seen as marking a break and turning-point in English history. J. D. Mackie, in his volume on *The Earlier Tudors* in the Oxford History of England (1952), reacted against this view: 'It is wrong to suppose that in the year 1485 any great change took place in the means whereby England was governed.' In his opening chapter, entitled 'The New Monarchy', he argued that a more gradual change was already under way. Mackie found the concept of the new monarchy useful, but he did not assert it as confidently as Pollard had done.

Since Mackie, historians of the Tudor period have tended to let the term 'new monarchy' slide into obscurity. This is in part because the focus of historical interest has shifted away from institutional and political matters to economic and social ones. More specifically, it is the result of forceful attacks on the validity and usefulness of the term. Its validity is, indeed, inherently suspect, because it is not a term contemporary with events, but an invented label. Its usefulness is limited by its elasticity. Historians have had conflicting ideas not only about the significance of the 'new monarchy', but about when it was initiated and developed. In the present discussion 1471 has been chosen as the starting-point because it has traditionally been regarded as the earliest date for its inception and because important developments in central government took place in the years following. For Pollard and his disciples the 1530s marked a decisive break, with the assertion of Henry VIII's Royal Supremacy over the church: only a mature new monarchy could have accomplished this. If the term as it has been applied has any historical validity, the construction of a new monarchy must be sought within the half century or so after 1471.

The matter is worth re-examining, because, despite the onslaughts on the concept of the new monarchy, it still hovers around works on sixteenth-century England. Its wraith-like presence has proved hard to exorcise, since it has been persistently linked with another concept, that of the 'Tudor century' (1485–1603), a categorization whose convenience has ensured its durability.

Moreover, some recent studies have shown Yorkist and early Tudor kings acting in ways compatible with the concept of a new monarchy. Alexander Grant has recently argued that 'the most important revolution in government of the period was surely the restoration of a high degree of peace and stability throughout most of the country, and its architect was King Henry VII. For this reason, his victory over Richard III in August 1485 deserves to be re-established as a major turning-point in English history' (1985). B. P. Wolffe, in his studies of the crown's lands and finances (1970, 1971), rehabilitated the playboy Edward IV as the king who, after his restoration in 1471, put the administration of royal estates on a different basis, providing himself and his successors with a more assured means of raising sizeable sums from their customary sources of revenue.

3

J. R. Lander demonstrated (1976) how Henry VII in his later years attempted to control the higher nobility by imposing fines and the making of bonds on them when they infringed statutes. There have been revealing studies of public ceremonies and court festivities by S. Anglo (1969), R. Strong (1973) and G. Kipling (1977). They have shown how under Henry VII and Henry VIII pageantry and spectacle projected the glory of the monarchy in new ways.

These developments in the spheres of finance, political relationships and propaganda had precedents and can be regarded as random facets of policy. However, J. R. Lander believes that changes in policy under the Yorkists and early Tudors were sufficiently notable and consistent for them to be bracketed under the heading of the 'new monarchy', which was not, he says, 'as some textbooks still imply, the same thing as the modern state . . . it was the seventeenth, not the fifteenth century that, in England, saw the end of the transition from the medieval to the modern state' (1977). Lander considers the essence of the new monarchy to have been a more effective application of existing royal powers, in response to a demand for more stable government. This the prince alone could satisfy, 'through a nice balance of reward and fear'. So there occurred in the later fifteenth century shifts in perceptions of the role which the prince should play: government was modified to meet the need.

Such developments have been seen as European ones. Indeed, the first historian to focus attention on the practical ways by which princes could increase their power was an Italian writing in the early sixteenth century. Niccolò Machiavelli, in *The Prince*, the little distillation of his political wisdom which he wrote in 1513, concerned himself above all with the problem of how the *parvenu* or usurping prince could impose and sustain a novel authority (1961). Machiavelli considered that he was establishing and elaborating eternal rules of political behaviour and prudent government; he did not believe that there was anything new about the sort of policies devised by successful rulers in his own day to attain power and sustain their dominance. But he pointed out how some recent Italian rulers had been able to establish their absolute rule speedily, and how the power wielded by some other hereditary princes, such as Ferdinand of Aragon and Louis XII of France, had come to overshadow European politics.

The rise of more powerful and highly centralized principalities has been seen by modern historians as a phenomenon of the period. In the words of J. H. Elliott, it was 'an age in which such forceful monarchs as Henry VIII of England or Louis XI of France [died 1483] consolidated the power of the Crown and devoted their efforts to the creation of a unified and centralised State under royal control' (1963). According to J. H. Shennan 'the figure of the secular ruler ... took on a new lease of life and, at the expense of alternative political forms, imposed his own authority' (1974). There was a 'renaissance of princely power'. H. G. Koenigsberger argued (1971) that such achievements were possible because of the dissolution of the feudal ties which had hitherto set the pattern of relations between princes and the higher and lesser nobility; and because of the development of a more sophisticated money and credit economy, which the former could exploit to raise money by taxation and loans on an unprecedented scale. Rulers could win loyalties more widely and fully by using their new resources to fund patronage. They came to stand 'at the centre of a nationwide network of patron–client relationships'. Impelled by the need to bind their subjects more firmly to their allegiance, princes expanded their jurisdictions and resources – domestically by extending the competence of their courts and bringing the church more fully under control, and abroad by acquiring new territories. These policies necessitated changes in the machinery of government: 'On this very general level of historical analysis there is some justification for the traditional term "the new monarchies".'

But Koenigsberger warns that, though monarchies increased their political and military power, they did not create modern states. Their over-ambitious policies in the long run sapped what effectiveness their bureaucracies had. Elites were able to exploit royal authority to line their pockets and resist its further encroachments. In the case of Spain, often cited as the classic example of the emergence of a new princely power in the period, J. H. Elliott has argued that the achievement was a limited one. Isabella of Castile and Ferdinand of Aragon, who united their kingdoms in 1479, created by the early sixteenth century 'a state far more subordinate at every level to royal authority than they had found'. But if 'the introduction of administrative uniformity and the centralising of power in the monarch's hands were essential features of the Renaissance State, the Spain of Ferdinand and Isabella would scarcely seem to qualify' (1963).

Thus historians of Europe have detected a qualitative change in the nature of princely governments in the later fifteenth and early sixteenth centuries. They are more ready than most historians of England to accept the continued use of terms such as the 'new monarchy' and the 'renaissance state'. Like Lander, they do not equate these with the emergence of the modern state. But in European historiography the spirit of Pollard, who was keenly aware of the European dimensions of the new monarchy concept, lives on.

Criticisms of New Monarchy Theories

A frontal assault was launched on the concept of the new monarchy in its English context by G. R. Elton in 1953 in a review of Mackie's 1952 volume in the Oxford History. 'We have come to realise', Elton wrote, 'that Yorkist or Tudor monarchy was nothing fresh either in aims or methods or doctrine.' Elton declared that the term new monarchy 'only confuses and ought to be abolished' (1953a). What he believed was that in the 1530s there occurred with remarkable rapidity profound changes in the nature of the English polity. The sovereignty of the king in parliament was more fully asserted, and implemented through the vigour of reformed or new central agencies of government. These achievements were above all the result of Thomas Cromwell's revolutionary concept of the nature of secular authority, and his ability to create clearly defined administrative structures to replace the traditional, less differentiated initiatives of the king and officers in his household. Elton thus retained the view that there was a decisive phase in the development of the modern state during the Renaissance period, but he shifted its point of departure forward from the restoration of Edward IV in 1471 or the battle of Bosworth in 1485 to the appointment of Cromwell as King's Secretary in 1534. Elton's classic exposition of these views is to be found in *The Tudor Revolution in Government* (1953b). Here he summarizes Cromwell's achievement:

> The plain fact is that Henry VII ascended the throne of a medievally governed kingdom, while Elizabeth handed to her successor a country administered on modern lines. In the course of this transformation there was created a revised machinery of government whose principle was bureaucratic organisation in place of the personal control of the king, and national management rather than management of the king's estate.

These conclusions have altered scholars' perceptions of the

6

'Tudor century's' place in the evolution of the English state, but some have vigorously objected to them. S. B. Chrimes concluded that 'it would be a grave mistake to imagine that the early modern system [of government] of the Tudors and Stuarts represented a fundamental departure from the medieval system' (1972). Another medieval historian, G. L. Harriss, had already subjected Elton's argument to a detailed critique (1963). Harriss objected to the notion of 'a swift and fundamental revolution in the nature of the state at the Henrician Reformation'. He argued that major advances for the claims of the unitary state which, according to Elton, were made then 'had been conceded in the course of the two preceding centuries', and that royal government in the century 1350–1450 was 'at once national and (in Dr Elton's terminology) "bureaucratic" '.

Writing in the same issue of *Past and Present*, Penry Williams viewed the institutional innovations of the 1530s as less innovatory and lasting than Elton, but nevertheless as a notable phase along with several others in a Tudor trend to establish a more bureaucratic government: 'the emergence of modern national government can be told neither in exclusively "revolutionary" nor in exclusively "evolutionary" terms.' Nor, according to Williams, was it established in the sixteenth century:

> The state which emerged in the later Stuart period admittedly owed much to the middle ages and much to the Tudors, but in many ways it was new and revolutionary. Permanent officials were appearing to control the army and the navy; the judiciary was no longer the prime arm of government; the treasury developed as a body separate from and superior to the exchequer; and the crown found itself able to raise sums in taxes and in loans that bore a nearer relationship to the national wealth (1963).

Recently, a group of Tudor historians have questioned aspects of Elton's thesis. In the conclusion to *Revolution Reassessed*, D. Starkey criticizes the view that early Tudor governmental change was the result of long-term planning and takes a more 'evolutionary' view: 'The 1530s have lost their primacy . . . And with the primacy of the 1530s goes much of Cromwell's personal role' (1986b).

Historians continue to regard the Yorkist and early Tudor period as particularly significant in the development of the authority of the state, but they disagree about the pace of changes and how fundamental they were. The proliferation of fifteenth-century studies has led to an insistence that central government did not break down in the Wars of the Roses. Medievalists have emphasized that the nation-state had old roots and was not an invention of the Yorkists and Tudors in response to these wars. Even the institutional effects of the Reformation on the monarchy can be seen, from a medieval perspective, as part of a long-maturing process. This re-assessment has tended to undermine the idea that there was a 'new monarchy'. For Harriss, the government of the Yorkists and Henry VII has elements of aberrant obsolescence rather than of novelty: its administration 'appears as a regression to an earlier form of government, conducted in the interests of the king and operating through his household' (1963). Elton's 'big bang' thesis thoroughly explodes the new monarchy. How, then, can we categorize the monarchy of the period 1471–1534? Can this be regarded as a distinct phase in its development? Did its kings have a conscious policy of introducing new constitutional and institutional arrangements? Did their policies increase the authority and power of the state in new ways?

Later Medieval Monarchy: Prerogative and its Limitations

Before examining how far the institutions of government changed in our period, it is necessary to examine the current views of the nature of monarchy at the start of it. For the concept of new monarchy implies the existence of a need to restructure the institution and a consciousness of its defects.

Since the twelfth century there had been a lively debate, in England as in other parts of western Christendom, about monarchy and its powers, and about the rights ('liberties') of subjects and whether they might overthrow a tyrant. There was general agreement that the royal 'estate' was an office ordained by God to fulfil specific functions in Christian society. Sir John Fortescue, Chief Justice of the King's Bench to Henry VI, succinctly put it like this: 'Though the king's estate be the highest estate temporal in the earth, yet it is an office in which he ministreth to his realm defence and justice' (1885). Monarchies were viewed as constituent parts in the temporal world of the Church Universal: they were parts of a unity whose higher orders were in the Heavenly Host.

In this context the role of monarchy was defined in a famous and controversial papal Bull, *Unam Sanctam*, promulgated by Pope Boniface VIII in 1302. He asserted (summarizing the pronouncements of many of his predecessors) that God had confided both spiritual and temporal authority to the papacy. God intended that popes should always exercise the superior, spiritual power, but that princes should normally exercise the lesser, temporal power, though subject to the judgment of the superior, the papacy. Popes therefore had the right to judge kings who erred. In 1516 Pope Leo X confirmed this bull. Medieval princes accepted that they were answerable to God for the conduct of their office, and that the papacy had a unique spiritual jurisdiction – hence Henry VIII's dependence on the papal court for judgment on his suit for the nullification of his marriage to Catherine of Aragon. But they jibbed at the proposition that popes had the right to condemn them and their rule. They insisted that they had 'imperium' within their realms, sovereignty in secular affairs, derived directly from God.

In practice ideological conflicts between popes and kings were exceptional, for their confrontations seldom reached such a pitch. English kings had even taken advantage of the political problems of the papacy in the fourteenth century in order to restrict the exercise of its spiritual authority, where this proved inconvenient for the crown. The Statutes of Praemunire enacted by parliaments of Edward III in 1353 and Richard II in 1393 opposed suit in the papal court of cases cognizable in the king's courts. This legislation constituted a long-standing grievance of the papacy against the crown. In 1426 Pope Martin V complained that it 'produces a kind of separation between England and the rest of the Church'. Nevertheless, the crown tended to respect papal spiritual rights, which were often used to its advantage. In practice, the papacy was prepared to co-operate with kings in the government of the English church, particularly as regards the important issue of the appointment of bishops.

When Henry VIII became Supreme Head of the English church, he was assuming a daring extension of royal authority and endowing the crown with a novel vicariate. Previous royal attacks on papal spiritual authority, and the degree of control which the crown exercised over spiritual affairs did not provide adequate precedents. Yet it was not new for English kings to assert that their estate had a unique religious position. Their right to hedge papal powers and to exercise authority over clerical as well as lay affairs had long been bolstered by religious ceremonies and myths.

The most important of these ceremonies was the coronation in Westminster Abbey, in which through the anointing with holy oil the king received divine grace and a semi-priestly character. He also received strength by the invocation of his predecessor St Edward the Confessor (ruled 1042–66, canonized 1161), whose magnificent shrine was in the abbey. In the coronation ceremony, St Edward's Crown (probably one actually used by the king) was placed on the king's head. Kings appeared arrayed in their holy glory, wearing their crowns, in religious ceremonies on the principal Christian festivals. These 'crown-wearings' were certainly still being held in the 1440s.

Thereafter kings continued to display the numinous power which they had received at the coronation by acting as healers. They 'touched for the evil' – applying through their hands miraculously curative powers to sufferers from skin diseases. On Good Friday they offered on the altar gold and silver coins which they would take back to be made into rings. These 'cramp rings', through the royal numinous power, could alleviate muscular spasms and pains, and were more specially efficacious in the treatment of epilepsy. When subjects addressed kings in reverent style and made ritual obeisances on meeting them, they were honouring the holy nature and power of kingship. By extension certain representations of the king as well as his person were deemed sacred. Men sometimes knelt to kiss his image on the seals attached to his letters. The screen set up in York Minster to flank the processional entrance to the choir in Henry VI's reign has statues of the king and his predecessors back to William the Conqueror, standing at the sacred portal as if they were saints. Devotees of the dead Henry treated his statue there and coins with his image on them as cult-objects: they 'bent a penny' in honour of King Henry when taking a vow to him. It has been suggested by S. Anglo that, in one of the London pageants for the reception of Catherine of Aragon in 1501, God the Father 'rejoiced in the visage and general appearance of Henry VII' (1969).

As God's vicar in the discharge of temporal rule, the king was recognized as having a reserve of inalienable power which he could exercise on his own initiative. He had his 'liberty', as his subjects had theirs, his 'prerogatives' of exercising his sole will and grace. Theoretically the king could bestow many of the crown's offices and estates on whom he wished: in many cases kings did so contrary to the advice of their councillors and the wishes of powerful domestic interest groups. The king could promote the harsh enforcement of a multiplicity of statutes; he could also issue dispensations from their operation to individuals and pardons for convictions to their transgressors. Royal ordinances were issued on his initiative without the advice and assent of parliament and might be enforced by his council through the imposition of crippling fines and imprisonment. The king was free to choose which foreign princes he wished to ally with or declare war on; his subjects commonly accepted the traditional obligations to give him military service, naval assistance and financial aid in defence of the realm and the crown's possessions annexed to it, in Wales, Scotland, Ireland and France.

The later medieval English monarchy was, therefore, accorded by its subjects a status which was holy and prestigious, and theoretical powers which might be used tyrannically. Arguably it had sufficient powers and did not need to be reshaped constitutionally as a new monarchy. This viewpoint is implicit in the writings of Sir John Fortescue. He argued, after personal experience of the collapse of Henry VI's rule, that there was no need to introduce a more authoritarian regime to heal recent political ills. He considered that the crown had the ability to cure its enfeeblement. Fortescue's prescription was the reformation of the royal finances and council on traditional lines (1885).

Fortescue's views on the nature of the English monarchy – which continued to be influential in the sixteenth century – reflected the existence of a strong and traditionally inclined 'public opinion' constituted chiefly by the propertied elites of gentlefolk, merchants and townsmen, but by no means confined to them. This public opinion possessed strong views about the manner in which kings should conduct their holy office. Key points were summed up by Fortescue: the king, he said,

> cannot at his pleasure change the laws of his kingdom . . . the statutes of England are established not only by the prince's will but by the assent of the whole kingdom . . . the king of England does not by himself or his ministers impose on his subjects any tallage [arbitrary tax] or burden, nor change their laws nor make new ones, without the express consent or concession of his whole kingdom in his parliament (1949).

In the coronation oath, the king swore to maintain the laws and do justice . There was the expectation that he would use his prerogatives in the interests of the common good ('commonwealth'). He ought not to be extortionate, or partial in the provision of justice. He ought not of his sole authority to deprive individuals of their rights under the common law. He should not act on important issues involving his own or the realm's interests without the advice and assent of respected councillors. A king should not alienate the inherited lands of the crown or lavish rewards and offices on the unworthy (for instance, the lowborn, foreigners, women). Therefore, though public opinion favoured a wide prerogative, contrarily it attempted to lay down narrow guidelines for its exercise, some embodied in parliamentary practices, others a matter of convention and sentiment.

Fortescue's insistence that England was not an absolute monarchy, but one in which the king exercised the power to make laws and raise taxes only in parliament, is a remarkable testimony to the strength of opinion, especially since he was a royal servant writing in the first instance for royal personages. At the start of our period the role of monarchy was thus authoritatively regarded, from a constitutional viewpoint, as fixed and unalterable, untramelled in important respects and restricted in others. In fact Fortescue, in his praise of royal prerogative, was playing the courtier: others were more suspicious of its threat of arbitrary government. The most popular native saint, Thomas Becket, was renowned as the victim of royal tyranny, a martyr for the liberty of the church. The lessons of Magna Carta were well remembered, and would not, as Pollard suggested (1910), be forgotten in the sixteenth century. Disgruntled subjects customarily tried to reconcile defiance of the royal will with the respect due to the king by blaming 'misgovernment' or 'evil counsellors'. Common folk banded together on occasion in protest against what they considered to be royal oppressiveness in raising war taxes, even when parliamentary sanction for grants made them lawful. In 1489 popular protests about subsidy in Yorkshire mushroomed into a momentarily formidable rebellion. In 1497 an army of Cornish peasants protesting about the subsidy grant encamped on Blackheath, threatening London and requesting the punishment of 'evil' councillors. In 1525 formidably large East Anglian demonstrations against the extra-parliamentary tax devised by Wolsey, the so-called 'amicable grant', led to its abandonment. English people were sensitive to the threat of harsh royal financial demands; they were set in their ways and suspicious of innovation. Any king who might have attempted in the later fifteenth and early sixteenth centuries to create a new monarchy based on the overthrow of the constitutional parameters trenchantly outlined by Fortescue faced the possibility of opposition from illiterate as well as educated opinion.

But, as Fortescue was at pains to point out, this constitutionalism had not stifled monarchical power. Englishmen revered their kings, wanted them to govern firmly and accorded them wide powers to do so. But they were intensely opinionated about how kings should govern. They kept alive a traditional hatred of tyranny, and their communities in shire and parliament could act as intense, obstinate political caucuses putting pressure on the crown, or resisting pressure from it.

The traditionalism of English political attitudes to royal power and their contradictoriness were at times irksome and dangerous for kings. They and their subjects might perceive the need for institutional change, but, as Fortescue insisted, in England this must be done under the guise of renovation, and without manifest prejudice to existing constitutional relationships between crown and community. If kings did feel the need to set up a new monarchy, it would have been imprudent to have advertised the intention; if they felt they had succeeded in doing so, equally imprudent to have advertised the fact.

2 The Development of Royal Administration

The Council and the Secretary

Protagonists of new monarchy theories concentrated attention on changes in the institutions of central government, which supposedly increased the prince's control over society. The evolution of princely bureaucracies remains a central theme in evaluations of how effectively the authority of the state developed in Europe in the sixteenth and seventeenth centuries. In this general European context particular emphasis has been laid on the appearance of the 'council of state' and the 'secretary of state' as among the most important instruments of governmental control. The significance of their particular evolution in England has been a matter of debate. The disappearance of many conciliar registers and records, particularly those dating from the second half of the fifteenth century, has made it difficult to relate the sixteenth-century council to its antecedents.

By the fifteenth century the royal council had a clearly defined membership and customary rules and habits of business. It concerned itself with a wide range of national and international affairs. The council was the main clearing-house of administration, settling such matters as the terms of appointments to office and of the tenure of grants; measures to finance and supply the maintenance of garrisons and the conduct of military and naval operations; the tenor of instructions to royal lieutenants and ambassadors. The council considered suits involving the crown's rights and concerning various sorts of public disorder, and petitions for justice from subjects and aliens. A council meeting might deal with a variety of business, judicial as well as advisory and administrative.

Normally councillors were appointed and dismissed by the king at will. They took oaths of loyalty and secrecy and received some remuneration for their work. Sessions were held several days a week in Westminster Palace during the terms of the nearby central law courts. Kings liked to have councillors at court; when the court was not at Westminster, some of them, forming the 'council attendant', might meet in a country palace out of term-time, or concurrently with their colleagues meeting separately at Westminster. The council had its own secretariat, headed by the clerk of the council, who kept its records (registers noting attendances, agenda and decisions).

The king himself sometimes presided at council meetings. Henry VII was an assiduous president, but other kings habitually remitted matters generally or a particular issue to whichever councillors were appropriate or available, for examination and termination by them, or for their advice on which policies might be followed or how policies might be implemented. Leading royal officials were *ex officio* councillors, such as the Chancellor, Treasurer of the Household, Keeper of the Privy Seal and judges and principal law officers. Secular peers figured prominently as councillors: they – especially the most eminently titled and wealthy among them – were considered to be the king's 'natural' councillors. The influence of such magnates on the council was sometimes viewed as politically threatening and unwelcome. But, like kings, they tended to be occasional in attendance. There was often an 'inner ring' of councillors who did most of the business, among whom royal officials predominated.

In composition, powers and functions the council under the Yorkists and up to the mid-1530s remained in many respects in a traditional mould, but the amount of conciliar business grew and there were the beginnings of important structural changes. The numbers appointed as councillors increased under Edward IV and Henry VII. Under Henry there was a proliferation of conciliar tribunals concerned with the adminis- tration of justice and the enforcement of royal rights. These tribunals disappeared, some permanently, in the reaction against his methods of rule early in his son's reign.

The youthful Henry VIII relied heavily in policy-making on an inner ring of mature peers and ministers, but Wolsey took over its policy-making role when he was chancellor (1515–30). Then, as J. A. Guy has shown (1977), the councillors, still numerous, were heavily engaged at Westminster in dealing with the huge amount of judicial business which Wolsey encouraged to be brought before the council. Wolsey also set up committees of councillors to deal with the flood of suits.

After Wolsey's fall there once more emerged an inner ring of councillors, working out the policy of the king's divorce, and of the campaign against the papacy. The distinction between such a group and the larger number of less crucial and distinguished councillors was to be finally institutionalized in 1540, when the Books of Acts of the Privy Council started to be compiled. The Privy Council was a body of fewer than twenty councillors, mostly leading royal officials, which met every day at court and monopolized the settlement of matters of high policy. Other councillors, occupied in routine chores, were distinguished as 'ordinary' councillors or 'councillors at large'. The judicial functions of the council were also more fully institutionalized in a separate structure. The privy councillors, with the judges (and, for a time, some of the lesser councillors), sat as the Court of Star Chamber, which had its own secretariat and registers distinct from those of the Privy Council.

This restructuring was above all the work of Thomas Cromwell, who managed the council during his ascendancy as secretary of state, and made the secretaryship the chief executive office of government. The office of king's secretary had emerged as an important one in the later fourteenth century. The secretary and his private office of clerks resided in the household and drafted the king's correspondence. This included letters to fellow princes and to nobles, and warrants which activated administrative action by central government offices – the Chancery, Exchequer and Privy Seal. The secretary was the keeper of the king's personal warrant, the signet seal, with which royal letters were authenticated. His habitual contact with the king might make him influential. Cromwell, however, used the secretaryship in an entirely new way – as the principal executive office through which he enforced and extended his control of government, central and local (1534–40). The clerks in his offices dispatched a mass of instructions on the king's behalf which went directly to the council, nobles and a host of royal officials. After his fall from power the secretaryship continued to be the chief office of state initiating policy and its implementation, in close conjunction with the Privy Council; two secretaries were to be appointed. These institutions were at the heart of Elizabethan and early Stuart government.

In many respects the council in the period 1471–1534 was an efficient version of a traditional institution, helping to reassert monarchical power. But the development of a number of conciliar tribunals was a novelty, suggesting a willingness in governing circles to adapt and extend the workings of the council in order to ensure a more efficient enforcement of royal rights and public order, and better provision for the resolution of politically troublesome tensions and disputes by the king's leading officials. Administrative developments in some respects foreshadowed the restructuring of the council initiated by Thomas Cromwell, which gave the crown more clearly defined executive institutions, whose relative efficiency is reflected in the crown's dependence on them for a century after 1540.

The Royal Household and the King's Finances

The household and its residences provided for the material needs of the king and those staying with him either semi-permanently or temporarily – close kinsfolk, nobles, retainers, foreign guests. But it provided much more than that, both for the king and those who sought his favour, refracting royal power in both symbolic and practical ways. Its luxurious ambience and settings and its solemn or joyful ceremonial occasions advertised the majesty of kingship. It was a centre of political and administrative activity whose repercussions might affect the whole realm and the king's possessions beyond it.

As the sounding-board for the projection of majesty, the household traditionally exhibited the holiness, wealth and power of the monarchy, in the magnificence of its religious processions and services in the chapel royal on important feast days, its outstandingly luxurious palaces, furnishings, plate and banquets, and in the number and distinction of its attendants and guests. The households of the Yorkists and early Tudors were notable for the revival of court splendour, somewhat neglected by the austere and withdrawn Henry VI. There were new building works and lavish entertainments. Masques were introduced under Henry VII and, in his son's court, became a favourite and even more elaborate pastime. These were tableaux in which allegorical scenes and incidents were staged, often on classical themes, with poetry, music and dance. The courtiers sometimes dressed up exotically to take part – and so did Henry VIII himself.

This new extravagance increased household expenses, the biggest normal charge on the king's ordinary revenues, and long a matter for concern in the political community. Fears had often been expressed in the fourteenth and fifteenth centuries that the king's substance was being wasted and greedily devoured at court, so that he could not 'live of his own', but attempted to gain the goods of his subjects, to their impoverishment. Such traditional views about the rightfulness of the king sustaining government from his limited private means reflect the prevalence of an embryonic concept of the nature and needs of state authority. They were views which posed problems for kings and their councillors: how were economy and munificence to be reconciled? Guests and their attendant suites at court expected to be accommodated and entertained in a manner which they considered appropriate to their rank. The number of household servants tended to increase. In 1450 household personnel had swelled to over 800; in the early 1460s it was reduced to about 550, but by the early seventeenth century had risen to some 1,500. However, the Yorkists and Tudors were outstandingly successful in running a prestigious household and at the same time in providing for its costs without alarming and outraging their subjects.

The personal nature of monarchy continued to make the household the centre of a gravitational pull. Chief ministers and councillors, whose absence from court might detract from its importance, on occasion resided there as did others who were magnets for politicking and business, such as peers and the envoys of foreign principalities. Their attention was focused mainly on what went on in the Chamber, a suite of rooms in the king's palaces where he lived with his close kinsfolk. The Chamber was also the most prestigious department of the household, with its own staff, headed by the Lord Chamberlain, and its own finances, presided over by the Treasurer of the Chamber. The customary attendants on the king who held office in the Chamber (such as the Knights and Esquires of the Body) might have a political influence disproportionate to their status and rank. Some Chamber servants waited on the king's person, some were his companions at mass, at table, shooting at the butts or riding in the hunting field. Consequently they might be well placed to influence his distribution of patronage and his policies.

Chamber officials were therefore likely to be caught up (and not necessarily as pawns of ministers or magnates) in the relentless game of faction, played out partly in the ante-chambers and closets of palaces, sometimes even within the curtains of the king's bed. The state of political play might be signalled at the king's public appearances in court, in his choice of an arm to lean on or lips to kiss tenderly, sending reverberations throughout the realm, or, indeed, Christendom.

A feature of medieval royal government was that some of the personnel and institutions of the household played an important part in administration as well as politics. It was characteristic of a personal monarchy that some of the central institutions should be based in the household, as was the secretaryship, acting as the king's personal secretariat, until Cromwell made it a detached governmental office. This movement of an office 'out of court' was a typical cycle of development in English medieval institutions. The process of detachment had started with the expansion of central government in the twelfth and thirteenth centuries. As the business and record-keeping of an office grew, so the itineracy of the household became more inconvenient and irksome. The king himself often did not need or wish to be in daily personal contact with the offices. By the start of our period the Exchequer, Chancery, Privy Seal and Council had long had permanent premises at Westminster. For much of the year their officials were in close touch with the household and those of their chief officers or members currently resident in it, since the king regularly stayed in the adjacent 'privy palace', until its apartments were devastated by fire in 1512. By 1536 nearby York Place, former residence of the archbishops of York, was Henry VIII's principal residence in the London suburbs – renamed Whitehall Palace, and being rapidly and gaudily extended. The court's frequent residence at Whitehall emphasized both its separateness from and close relationship with government offices and courts down the road in what had become the administrative capital at Westminster.

But such a description of Westminster needs qualification. The household remained an important centre for the settlement of business by the king in collaboration with his ministers and councillors, and some of the household's officers continued to perform more general administrative tasks, either in conjunction with the Westminster offices or bypassing them. The fact that such offices had gone out of court, wholly or in part, led the king to rely on those around him to co-operate with them in administrative tasks or to perform these more expeditiously. The organization and functions of the household and the specialist skills of many of its officers made it an ideal base for the development of *ad hoc* administrative structures for more general purposes. For it was one of the oldest and most elaborate bureaucracies in existence, divided into departments with closely defined and interlocking responsibilities, which adhered to rigidly controlled financial procedures based on written accounts, and were staffed by specialist, graded officials.

It is a feature of our period that there were vigorous assertions of the household's role in administration, some of them novel in form and scope. In Edward IV's reign, particularly after his restoration in 1471, Chamber officials played a key role in the development of a type of land administration not hitherto generally used by the crown. The Treasurer of the Chamber began to receive the cash profits from receivers, salaried officials in charge of groups of estates in the king's hands; such properties had hitherto been leased out for rent under Exchequer control. The Treasurer now disbursed the cash for household expenses and for any other purpose that the king ordered. As David Starkey has written, 'The move from Exchequer to Chamber meant the replacement of decentralized debit finance with a highly centralized wholly cash-based fiscal system' (1986a). Groups of royal councillors were appointed to conduct an annual audit of the accounts of receivers and their subordinates; they also acted as a court settling estate business and policy. This financial system (similar to that used by magnates, such as on the private estates inherited by Edward IV) largely displaced the control of receipt and account exercised by the Exchequer over customary revenues.

The new system was to go a long way towards solving the monarchy's cash-flow problem, especially in relation to household costs. It provided centralized control easily overseen by the king and geared to augmenting revenue. Though Henry VII at first rejected all this (presumably regarding it as a Yorkist aberration) and restored Exchequer authority, by 1491 he had reinstated the Chamber's role as an independent financial institution. The auditing and judicial activities of the conciliar committee (the King's General Surveyors) helped to increase exploitation. By the end of the reign the Treasurer of the Chamber, John Heron, whose accounts were audited by the businesslike Henry, had become the principal receiver and spender of royal revenues. In 1509, says Penry Williams (1979), the land revenues were up to £42,000 per annum, four times the level of 1433. The total ordinary revenue of the crown in 1509 was probably about £113,000 (£40,000 of it from the customs). This cash total was much greater than the amount which the Lancastrian kings had had at their disposal.

G. R. Elton, B. P. Wolffe and D. Starkey have traced ways in which this financial system was eroded and lost momentum in Henry VIII's reign. From 1509, according to Wolffe (1970, 1971), there was a steep decline in the contribution of land revenues to national finances, initially attributable to hostility both in council and parliament to the powers exercised without statutory basis by the General Surveyors. These were gradually restored, but the General Surveyors did not have the same scope as hitherto. Under Wolsey's chancellorship the demands of war produced an emphasis on seeking revenue by extraordinary levies; customary income was insufficient. Cromwell also sought additional revenue in the 1530s from the seizure of ecclesiastical lands and incomes; as Elton has shown (1953b), he set up a series of revenue courts distinct from the household to handle these and the older customary sources of income.

Recently Starkey has demonstrated how developments in household organization under Henry VII and Henry VIII affected financial organization and politics (1986a). By the mid-fifteenth century the Chamber was divided into a suite of apartments used for public ceremonies and a suite where the king lived – the Secret or Privy Chamber. Starkey notes that Henry VII excluded the authority of the Lord Chamberlain from the Privy Chamber, which thus became a largely autonomous household department staffed by grooms and pages, headed by the Groom of the Stool, whose formal office was the care of the king's portable lavatory. Responsibility and influence gravitated to those close to the king. The Groom of the Stool under Henry VII came to handle the king's personal finances and to be free from dependence on the Treasurer of the Chamber for funds. The growing influence of the Privy Chamber staff was reflected in Wolsey's interventions – from 1513 the Groom once more drew his funds from the Treasurer, and in 1519 the cardinal procured the appointment of attendants to replace the young cronies surrounding Henry. By 1520 these officers had the more exalted title of 'Gentleman of the Privy Chamber'.

After Wolsey's fall in 1529 the Privy Chamber gained a temporary primacy in royal finance: the Privy Purse now handled the king's personal expenses and the costs of policy, receiving its funds from the Privy Coffers, a number of treasuries kept in the king's palaces, instead of by block grants from the Treasurer of the Chamber. It was this interlocking system of Privy Purse and Privy Coffers, Starkey argues, which eclipsed the role of the Chamber in national finance, rather than the rise of Cromwell's informal treasurership and of the revenue courts – though these developments were to undermine the key role of the Privy Purse. But much of the money collected in Henry's later years ended up in the Privy Coffers, essentially a household treasury:

> the treasury was … since Henry handled much of the money himself and kept it, if not under the bed, at least at the back of his bedchamber in the secret jewel house, a dramatic reassertation of the vitality of household administration. (Starkey, 1986a)

This complex story of financial administration, with its disputed interpretations, at least clearly shows that the period was one of adaptability and experiment in institutional developments. The Yorkists and Henry VII reinforced the traditional import-ance of the household in administration. Household departments played novel parts in controlling ordinary revenues, helping to increase efficiency. The crown's hitherto dismal financial position was transformed. In the 1530s and 1540s further institutional changes undermined the dominance of household departments in financial administration. As J. D. Alsop has written of this development, 'what was innovatory was an arrangement of crown finance founded upon the proliferation of autonomous courts.' The direction of finances was to gravitate from individual ministers, household officers and groups of councillors more firmly into the hands of the council: 'It was only in the early 1540s that the Council emerged as an authoritative institution with a general collective competence and jurisdiction in financial administration, complete with the power to issue its own warrants for the expenditure of crown money' (Alsop 1986).

Customary revenues were supposed to cover the crown's normal running expenses – the household, officers' wages, annuities and presents, the costs of building and peacetime defence works, embassies, the king's personal expenditure and the purchase of luxury and other items. For abnormal expenses in emergencies – the costs of campaigns and of wartime defences – kings had the right to call on the financial aid of their subjects.

Henry VIII's government was faced by the problems of rising normal expenditure and enormous burdens from the costs of warfare – in the period 1512–17 the latter amounted to about £900,000. Cromwell's augmentations of customary revenue in the 1530s did not suffice to cover customary expenditure. As Alsop has shown (1982), the government was in the habit of applying the profits of taxation to normal as well as abnormal expenditure. Though its principal justification for raising subsidies remained necessity in emergencies, in the middle decades of the century it was moving towards the position that taxation was justified to maintain the crown.

There were several ways in which kings customarily raised taxes. There were extra-parliamentary levies – interest-free loans and goodwill gifts ('benevolences') which individuals and communities were pressured into making. These were highly unpopular and widely regarded as unconstitutional. The most brazen example of an attempt to raise benevolences in the period was the 'amicable grant', a charge on income which Wolsey tried to impose in 1525. Then there were subsidies ('tenths and fifteenths') granted in parliament primarily by the Commons. The shires' various contributions to these had long been fixed: the grant of one tenth and one fifteenth yielded the relatively modest national total of about £35,000. Penry Williams has outlined how in the period 1513–16 the crown extracted parliamentary subsidies (in addition to these old-fashioned, low-yield ones) which were based on direct assessments of individual wealth (1979). Since the later fourteenth century, government had experimented with new forms of parliamentary taxation. But it was only in Henry VIII's reign that the crown succeeded in getting a more lucrative type of subsidy accepted as a norm. This was a remarkable success in tapping the wealth of the nation more realistically. The new-style subsidies helped Henry VIII to maintain large-scale wars up to the end of his reign and were to provide Queen Elizabeth with the means to sustain warfare, with Spain, over a longer period than at any time since the Hundred Years War.

To conclude: in our period the royal household continued to fulfil its traditional tasks as the provider of the king's personal needs and reflector of his majesty. These long outlasted the period, as did the household's role as a centre of political life. This role, indeed, fluctuated in importance according to the personality and will of the king. Henry VII rigidly controlled competitive elements among his courtiers. There were times in Henry VIII's reign when the gentlemen of his Privy Chamber exercised a strong influence on policy-making and patronage; at other times power gravitated to the households of the chief ministers, Wolsey and Cromwell.

Traditionally, the household played a pivotal part in royal administration, again varying according to the character of the monarch. B. P. Wolffe has shown (1970, 1971) how the

23

households of the Yorkist kings and Henry VII came to absorb revenue administration – their comprehensive control of customary revenues – an achievement for which it is difficult to find earlier parallels. Much of the financial gain was in the long run to prove disappointing; from Henry VIII's reign onwards the crown's dependence on taxation was once more heavy. But in this sphere, by process of trial and error, the crown gradually notched up important political gains. The subsidy experiments of the 1510s provided a lasting and more lucrative basis of taxation, and by the end of the reign the crown had heavily eroded the principle that taxation could be raised only for emergencies.

It is remarkable that the Commons in parliament granted huge sums to Henry VIII with so little protest and acquiesced in the application of national wealth to the costs of government more fully than had been customary. This relative docility can perhaps be attributed to a changing climate of opinion among the elites, an altered perception of their duties as subjects towards the prince. Criticism of royal extravagance and financial competence, a significant political trend in the century or so before Edward IV's financial reforms, faded. The vigour and success of Yorkist and Tudor financial policies were an important element in changing attitudes towards the monarchy.

The Provision of Justice

Kings by virtue of their office were the supreme secular judges in the realm, and, by virtue of various princely titles annexed to the kingship, in their other lordships in the British Isles and France. They often demonstrated this crucial aspect of kingship by presiding when lawsuits were heard in council and parliament. It was the king's responsibility to ensure that royal judges upheld the common law and the statutes, to insist in royal ordinances on their strict enforcement, and to co-operate in parliament in the provision of new statutory remedies for current ills. The crown appointed many local judges (justices of the peace) as well as exalted central ones, the professional lawyers who presided in Westminster Hall over the King's Bench, which dealt mainly with the pleas of the crown, notably serious crimes (felonies), and over the Common Pleas, concerned with civil suits between subjects. Twice a year the Justices of the King's Bench perambulated the realm on allotted circuits, holding sessions in chief county towns. There, with the assistance of local juries and law enforcement officers, they presided at the assizes, settling civil and criminal actions, 'delivering' the county gaols by trying the prisoners, and dealing with cases of exceptional disorder under royal commissions of 'oyer et terminer' (to hear and conclude).

Much of the staple rural mayhem of trespass, assault and riot, and many cases of felony, never got as far as consideration by the judges of the King's Bench or by other central judicial tribunals, such as those composed of groups of the king's councillors. The main burden of keeping order in the shires fell on the justices of the peace in their regular and individual sessions. These groups of mostly amateur judges were appointed from time to time by the crown for each shire. Cities and boroughs, by virtue of their royal and baronial charters of privileges, had developed their own systems of courts, which tried to engross the judgment of crimes and civil disputes within urban boundaries and among their inhabitants, as well as enforcing economic regulations. There were also many 'private' courts with fixed boundaries and varying categories of jurisdiction, courts belonging in perpetuity to 'undying' ecclesiastical corporations (for instance, monasteries) or to noble families. These areas of jurisdiction were part of the patrimony of a religious community's presiding saint or of an aristocratic heir – his or her franchise, or 'liberty' or 'soke'.

Lords and ladies who possessed manors had the right to enforce the regulation of bread and ale prices in the manor court. In some of these courts they had jurisdiction over petty crime equivalent to that exercised by the court of the hundred. Hundreds (called 'wapentakes' in northern England) were the ancient administrative divisions of the shire. Some hundreds and their courts were, indeed, privately owned franchises, not part of royal jurisdiction. In such private franchisal courts, and in manor courts with fuller rights of jurisdiction, the lord's steward imposed sentences according to jury verdicts for a variety of public offences, in a session known as a 'court leet'.

There were in England a few very large private franchises. The largest were the duchy of Lancaster and the county palatine of Chester, comprising respectively Lancashire and Cheshire, both attached to the crown, and the bishopric of Durham (later County Durham). Other extensive ecclesiastical liberties were those of the abbeys of St Albans and St Edmunds (Bury St Edmunds, Suffolk) and the Soke of Peterborough Abbey. Now part of Northumberland are the bishops of Durham's former liberties of Bedlingtonshire, Norhamshire and Islandshire (Lindisfarne Island), the archbishops of York's liberty of Hexhamshire, and the crown's liberties of Tynedale and Redesdale. The greatest concentrations of 'liberties' held in heredity by English noble families were in the eastern and southern parts of Wales. Their government was separate and distinct from that of the principality of Wales, annexed to the crown. In these 'Marches of Wales' magnates who often combined Norman and Welsh descents exercised regal powers of criminal and civil jurisdiction, powers derived from those previously exercised by their princely Welsh predecessors.

The existence of extensive franchises in England and Wales in some cases restricted and in other cases complicated the exercise of royal justice, especially on the peripheries of the realm. Legal hedges and intense local partiality protected their inhabitants from suits promoted elsewhere or by outsiders. Welshmen from Marcher lordships traditionally had a bad name for lawlessness among their English neighbours, as did inhabitants of the more rugged Northumberland liberties generally in the Anglo-Scottish borders. All over England fugitives from suits in the central royal courts and from courts in shire, city and borough might evade pursuing officials by crossing into a liberty. The execution of justice in liberties depended on the variable zeal and control of the lords and their officers.

Churches too possessed a special franchise – the right of sanctuary. Suspected criminals were protected from arrest when they took refuge in churches. After forty days' residence there they had to surrender and either stand trial or swear before a coroner to leave the realm from the nearest port. Anyone of clerical estate enjoyed an important liberty – that of being handed over after a criminal conviction before secular judges for trial in an ecclesiastical court and the infliction of punishment by the ecclesiastical authorities, who could not impose or implement sentences involving the shedding of blood. This privilege (known as 'benefit of clergy') extended to those who were in minor orders, not fully priests: the sole test in the king's court of such clerical status was a demonstration of the ability to read a short text from Scripture in Latin, the aptly named 'neck' verse.

Starting in our period, the problems posed to the exercise of royal justice by the existence of this variety of privileges were tackled decisively by the monarchy, in ways which strengthened

26

and extended its authority and produced greater uniformity. The peripheries of the realm were brought more firmly under central control and the differentiated status of the inhabitants of liberties was eroded, making them more fully the king's subjects, answerable to his laws. These processes were erratic and to some extent fortuitous. Though recurring trends in policy-making can be seen, they cannot be regarded as facets of a coherent, long-term plan.

The process by which the crown's relations with the Welsh Marches were transformed, and their mode of government overhauled, was a lengthy one. Edward IV, in his capacity as Earl of March, inherited twenty-three Marcher lordships. As a result of his usurpation in 1461, they were annexed to the crown; neither he nor his successors were inclined to sever the connection. The council appointed in 1471 to administer the affairs of his infant son Edward (the future Edward V), on his creation as Prince of Wales, Earl of Chester and Duke of Cornwall, received in the prince's name in 1476 a general commission of oyer et terminer in the Marches and adjacent English shires. In 1477 the prince's council was given control of the Marcher lordships of the earldom of March and in 1479 of those of the earldom of Pembroke. Charles Ross (1974) wrote that the council gained 'a supervisory authority' in the Marches 'and in the border counties to deal with failures of justice or official negligence, as well as complete power in the principality, the earldom of March, and other lordships belonging to the Crown.' The council lapsed after Edward IV's death; it was revived in 1490 by Henry VII for his infant son Arthur, Prince of Wales, and continued after Arthur's death in 1502. In 1493 the prince had been given judicial powers similar to Prince Edward's – he was able to appoint commissions of oyer et terminer, to raise forces, and to inquire into liberties and fugitives. These were to be among the permanent powers of the Council in the Marches of Wales.

Henry VII did not aim to destroy the franchises of the Marcher lords; he wanted them to be more effectively policed. To this end he also entered into indentures with lords by which they promised to ensure justice. The task of supervising justice in the Marches was facilitated by the lapse through escheat and forfeiture of a large number of Marcher lordships into crown possession under Henry VII. In 1521 the last major group in private hands was forfeited as a result of Buckingham's treason. In 1534 the council was given statutory powers of jurisdiction over all the inhabitants of the principality and Marches. They were given the right to appeal to the council from judgments in Marcher lords' courts. Under this statute felonies committed in the lordships came within the purview of justices of gaol delivery and of peace in neighbouring English shires. Officers of the lordships were made responsible for the appearance of the accused before these royal justices.

There were both parallels and differences between the problems caused by the distinctive form of government in the Marches of Wales and the 'problem of the North'. In the North liberties were not universal, nor generally so independent of the crown's control. The problem of lawlessness was exacerbated by the region's greater remoteness from Westminster and proximity to an international frontier, and by the consequent strength of local sentiments, which focused patriotism on magnate families and saints' cults rather than the crown. The problem of northern lawlessness was an aspect of the crown's larger political problems, international as well as domestic. Edward IV had no new solution to 'the problem of the North'. He relied, like previous kings, on building up the provincial dominance of magnates. In 1471 he granted his brother Richard, Duke of Gloucester, the estates and offices which the latter's father-in-law, Warwick the Kingmaker, had held in the region, and in the 1470s strengthened his brother's position by granting him the keeping of the Duchy of Lancaster lordships in Yorkshire and other northern properties. Gloucester shared power with Henry Percy, Earl of Northumberland. As Charles Ross wrote, 'whether singly or in collaboration [they] had come to wield a quasi-royal authority in the north by the mid-seventies' (1974). This authority was exercised particularly through their private councils, before whom were summoned alleged peace-breakers and those willing to have their disputes resolved.

It was Gloucester's usurpation of the crown as Richard III which helped to replace magnate domination by a provincial royal council similar to the one which developed in Wales. As king he was determined that his now remote northern power-base should not succumb to the Earl of Northumberland's control. In 1484 he instituted a council, under the presidency of his nephew John de la Pole, Earl of Lincoln, which was to meet quarterly at York and was to keep the peace, punish lawbreakers, and take action on petitions in northern parts. The Council of the North was 'perhaps Richard's most enduring monument, for its jurisdiction and procedure remained largely unchanged until its dissolution in 1641' (Ross 1981). Wolsey in 1522 revived the lapsed council under the nominal presidency of Henry VIII's illegitimate son, the Duke of Richmond. By the end of the reign the council was exercising an extensive civil and criminal jurisdiction in the whole region north of the Humber, except in the duchy of Lancaster.

By then the privileges and jurisdiction of various sorts of franchises had been largely whittled away by statute. The special liberties appertaining to churches and protecting clerics had been curtailed. Restrictions were placed on the use of sanctuaries and on the right of appeal to benefit of clergy. In 1495 the notoriously lawless liberty of Tynedale had been annexed to Northumberland – this brought it within the sheriff's jurisdiction, but it was not an immediate solution to the problem. A statute of 1536 (Elton 1982) struck generally at franchisal jurisdictions. They were portrayed in it as unfortunate aberrations detracting from the unity of the state – a novel view, not a typically medieval one. It was stated that some of 'the most ancient prerogatives of justice appertaining to the imperial crown of this realm' had been severed from it by past royal grants of franchises 'to the great diminution and detriment of the royal estate of the same and to the hindrance and great delay of justice.' Sovereignty was indivisible: 'it shall be supposed anything to be done against the King's peace, shall be made and supposed to be done only against the King's peace, his heirs and successors, and not against the peace of any other person or persons.' In major matters the statute reduced the courts of franchises to executors of royal justice. Lords of franchises were deprived of the power to pardon serious offences and outlawries. Their courts were to be held only on the authority of royal letters patent; indictments in them were to be made in the king's name.

By statutes of 1536 and 1543 the Marcher lordships were replaced by shires: in this period the earldom of Chester took on the status of a shire. Cheshire and Lancashire retained their special 'palatine' courts; writs continued to run there respectively in the names of the Earl of Chester and Duke of Lancaster. The bishops of Durham remained *ex officio* justices of peace in the bishopric, and the archbishops of York in Hexhamshire. But these differentiating privileges were more matters of appearance than substance.

The early Tudors also brought a new vigour to the regulation of society through the general system of secular courts. At the end of the Tudor period the justices of the peace were responsible for enforcing 133 statutes made before 1485, and a further sixty added between then and the end of Henry VIII's reign. A stimulus to legislation, especially from the 1530s onwards, was an intensification of domestic problems, economic and social. The governors of society became increasingly alarmed at the destabilizing effects of depopulation, dearth and rising prices and thrust on the justices of the peace the task of implementing remedies and controlling the people. Many early Tudor statutes were, indeed, re-enactments (often with amplifications and modifications) of earlier legislation.

Enforcement remained a problem. 'Default of justice' was a traditional complaint against kings and their councillors – and one which had recently proved particularly dangerous to rulers. It was among the charges circulated in the 1440s and 1450s against the ministers of Henry VI. There were deep-seated problems in the operation of judicial institutions which frustrated litigants and facilitated and encouraged perversion of the law. The forms of summons and action in the central courts of King's Bench and Common Pleas had inadequacies and inflexibilities which were well tailored to legal chicanery, leading to delay or dismissal of a suit. Influence at the royal court could be sought to procure immunity from being sued or the grant of a pardon. The central courts' dependence on the verdicts of local juries laid the law open to other sorts of partial influence; litigants might procure local influence to intimidate or bribe jurors or the sheriff who selected them. Besides, judicial institutions in the localities were also vulnerable to abuse. The justice of the peace had powers to arrest, detain and bind over to keep the peace which he might use in a personal quarrel.

The entrenched habits of lawyers and landowners made it difficult for government to contemplate any considerable reform of public courts or reduction of their competence. Yorkist and early Tudor kings and councillors certainly showed a particular awareness of the need to ensure better order and justice. These ideals are implicit in a letter from Wolsey to Henry VIII: 'And for your realm our lord be thanked it was never in such peace nor tranquillity. For all this summer I have had neither of Riot, felony nor forcible entry, but that your laws be in every place indifferently ministered without leaning of any matter' (Guy 1977).

To achieve such ends, recourse was had to a variety of ministerial and conciliar tribunals, exercising aspects of the king's prerogative of expediting justice and sometimes receiving royal commissions or statutory authority to try certain categories of offences. By the Yorkist period the chancellor presided over his court of equity. Proceedings were initiated by bills addressed to him alleging default or perversion of justice in common law proceedings. The chancellor might intervene to modify or supplement proceedings in other courts; he might make a judgment himself, or persuade parties to agree to arbitration. Breaches of contract came to be an area where Chancery specialized in providing remedy. The court's effectiveness stemmed in part from its method of summons, by the powerfully backed writ of subpoena; its unrestricted verbal examinations of the parties and witnesses; and its readiness to examine all kinds of written evidence.

In our period there was a considerable increase in the court's business, as there was in the judicial activity of the king's council. Tribunals proliferated dealing with different sorts of business. The Yorkist kings had their 'court of requests' for disgruntled suitors trailing along behind the royal household, a court composed of household officials and councillors in attendance on the king. This was revived by Henry VII, and from the late 1510s became primarily a sedentary body meeting in Westminster during the terms of the central law courts. Henry VII statutorily constituted two conciliar tribunals empowered to implement Acts dealing with types of disorder and corruption. The first, established in 1487, was to consist of a leading group of councillors empowered to inflict punishments according to the common law for offences such as riot, illegal retaining, and perversion of justice. The second, established in 1495, was to deal with perjury in lawsuits. Both courts were abolished in the reaction after Henry's death against his government. But in 1529 the 1487 court was revived.

The most remarkable manifestation of the vigour and scope of conciliar justice in the period is to be found in the patchily surviving evidence of the Tudor council's exercise of its judicial functions at its meetings in its suite of offices at Westminster known as the Star Chamber. Here variable groups of councillors sat on an *ad hoc* basis, dealing with both criminal and civil cases. Proceedings before them were rarely initiated officially, but usually by a bill of complaint or written information from a private party. The council had been, as J. A. Guy has described (1977), traditionally a source of equitable remedy for acts contrary to public justice, such as corrupt verdicts by juries, maintenance and the misdoings of royal officials. It also had a statutory jurisdiction in cases of riot and public disorder. It did not deal directly with capital offences (treason and felonies) or the determination of land titles. The bulk of its cases in the early Tudor period were connected with disputes over property, brought to the council under the guise of complaints about public disorder.

The council summoned the defendant and witnesses by Chancery writ of subpoena; proceedings were carried on by means of written submissions and questioning. If the suit ended in a determination, a decree was issued by the chancellor. But in suits which were basically civil in character, proceedings were terminated by an expert opinion from judges and lawyers; otherwise, the suit was committed for settlement by a group of 'indifferent' arbitrators or (if the parties preferred it) to a group to devise an extra-legal compromise. For criminal offences the court imposed fines (as it did for contempt) and terms of imprisonment, in lieu of, or as a supplement to, fines. Sometimes it sentenced offenders to be pilloried or otherwise publicly shamed.

There was a dramatic increase of Star Chamber suits during Wolsey's chancellorship (1515–29). The readiness of the crown to receive suits was a boon to litigious gentlefolk, and it provided a peaceable arena in which the government could monitor and, indeed, attempt to manipulate local rivalries and disputes which otherwise might have escalated into violence and polarized gentlefolk and their dependents and 'well-willers' into factious affinities. Star Chamber justice was a safety valve for aristocratic tensions. At the council board, rivals could fight with their evidences rather than resorting to force and arms. By its novel readiness to encourage suits the crown increased its ability to pacify and regulate regional politics.

The judicial activities of chancellor, council and other groups of central royal officials had precedents. But in our period ministerial courts of justice became more numerous, more vigorous and wider in scope. Their history was by no means one of unbroken progression; some faltered and disappeared or lay moribund for long spells. Their development increased respect for the monarchy, enhanced its usefulness to subjects and strengthened its ability to enforce the royal will and defend royal interests. The monarchy's more dominant judicial primacy was also increased by the gradual decline and abolition of franchises and liberties, and the development of provincial royal courts. Though there were protests about the Crown's tyrannical application of the laws, the complaints which had grown in the fifteenth century that the Crown was not generally providing effective means of justice died down.

The Military Strength of the Crown

Throughout the period the crown continued to rely heavily for the forces which it needed to deploy at home, at sea and abroad on the kinds of military and naval services customarily given by its English subjects. There was the ancient obligation of able-bodied men between the ages of sixteen and sixty to keep arms and armour appropriate to their station and to be ready to muster when summoned, the common folk arraying for war under the command of their local constables in shire, city and borough. Commissions of array were appointed by the crown for each shire, to inspect the equipment of the levies and, in emergencies, to select the most able men for service and organize them in companies to march off to the encampment. Those not selected were taxed for contributions to the expenses of the levies. The arrayers comprised the sheriff, knights and other property-holders within the shire who had military experience. Urban authorities were responsible for raising their own levies to man their walls and gates, as well as to march out and join up with other arrayed contingents.

Special defence obligations were owed by those who lived near the realm's long coastlines and near its chronically disordered northern borders. Coastal dwellers had to maintain warning beacons and keep watch in emergencies. Inhabitants near the Scottish Borders were also obliged to light beacons warning of raids, and to 'follow the fray' – assist their neighbours when warning was given that an attack was in progress or had taken place. Many borderers owed defence service to their landlord under the terms of their tenancies, and, arrayed under him or the local land sergeant, would report for service to the King's Lieutenant in the Marches, the regional Warden, or their deputies.

Shire and urban levies were raised by commissions of array in 1536 to oppose the northern rebellions just as they had been in 1469–71 to support Edward IV and Henry VI against attempted overthrows. Early Tudor commissions and procla-mations demonstrate royal concern to maintain the preparedness of the customary levies. The common folk were exhorted to practise archery and eschew indulgence in useless and unruly pastimes such as football. The long-bow remained the missile weapon with which the commons could most easily equip and train themselves. The relatively new-fangled arquebus was expensive, and for effective deployment needed more complex drills. The crown continued to value highly its right to summon the militia, armed with bill (a curved blade projecting from the end of a long wooden shaft) or bow. The long-bowman, trained to the right pitch, was not obsolescent on the continental battlefield. Under Henry VIII attempts were made to assess the numbers of those who owed service and to improve their organization and quality. In 1522 commissioners for musters were ordered to return lists of recruits, as they were in 1539 and 1542.

The crown still relied heavily on individual peers and knights for the raising and command of contingents to the shire levies and armies abroad. Lieutenants and Wardens of Marches and captains of frontier fortresses were also men of high noble status who undertook to raise their own military retinues to fill up their commands. The retinues of magnates were conspicuous in the armies led from Calais to invade France – by Edward IV in 1475, Henry VII in 1492 and Henry VIII in 1513. As Penry Williams has shown (1979), in Henry VIII's last years the crown was still relying heavily on individual landowners to recruit contingents for service abroad. However, their obligation was becoming limited to recruitment, and the companies which they raised were being more fully integrated under royal command. For the Flanders campaign of 1543, liability for service was based on the information compiled in the muster-books, and the contingents were amalgamated on a county basis. Though the military leadership exercised by magnates over their tenants and neighbours was becoming simply a matter of organizing them for service, nobles still on occasion led the men in their lordship to war.

Thus the military power of the crown, heavily reliant on taxable subjects for finance and on individual nobles for deployment, fluctuated according to the needs of the moment and the goodwill of subjects. The Tudors found it financially and politically challenging to meet the costs of warfare, which were rising generally, and especially steeply in Henry VIII's reign. They could not afford to imitate the French royal custom of maintaining substantial standing forces. The professional soldiers employed by the English crown were numbered normally in hundreds rather than thousands, scattered in garrisons at the extremities of the realm and impossible to concentrate as a field force. There were the contingents in the castles of the March of Calais (principally at Calais, Guines, Hammes); there was the garrison at Tournai from 1513 to 1525. Carlisle was always garrisoned; so, after its recapture in 1482, was Berwick.

An innovation of the period was the attachment of a sizeable armed guard to the king's household. Henry VII formed that still existing body, the Yeomen of the Guard. The formation of such palace units reflects the insecurity felt by kings in the period as a result of unhappy personal experiences. Warwick the Kingmaker's supporters had seized an unprepared Edward IV in 1469; in another rebellion in 1470 Warwick's supporters had compelled Edward to flee abroad with a few companions. Henry VII seemed in dire peril in the north in 1486, when he and his unarmed household were confronted by rebellion in Yorkshire.

In a period when continental warfare exhibited a revised professionalism based on new tactics and technology, the English crown continued to rely heavily for internal security, the defence of the realm and for its expeditionary forces abroad on the traditional obligations and amateur skills of able-bodied subjects. Major changes in these conventions and methods would have been administratively difficult and politically dangerous. Henry VIII supplied his foreign expeditions with the specialist formations of pikemen and arquebusiers they needed by hiring companies of continental mercenaries. A developing branch of warfare in which the crown had long imported foreign expertise and also developed native ability was artillery. By the Lancastrian period the Master of the Ordnance was responsible for maintaining the royal artillery and for having shot and new guns cast and gun carriages constructed. The master's principal depot and factory was in the Tower of London. There his gunners supervised repair and manufacture by specialized workmen. Edward IV took at least thirteen heavy pieces of artillery on his invasion of France in 1475. Henry VIII's artillery proved its worth in France in 1513 by breaking up the attempt to relieve Thérouanne and in the bombardment of Tournai.

The increased activity of the Ordnance Office under the Tudors was reflected in the growing size of its personnel. Besides supplying siege and field artillery for the campaigns, it controlled the assignment of guns for the new-style emplacements added to royal castles particularly in Henry VIII's reign. These redoubts not only provided gun platforms, but made old-fashioned medieval high towers and walls more secure against bombardment. In the years 1539–47 vast sums were spent on building a string of up-to-date artillery forts along the southern and eastern coasts, some of which survive (for instance, at Falmouth, Camber, Deal and Walmer).

A sphere of war in which royal power grew under the Tudors was the naval one, stimulated by technological change and the new bouts of confrontation with France. Henry V had been the first king since the Norman Conquest to build up a substantial royal navy, about thirty ships by 1417, with an administrative organization under the Clerk of the King's Ships. But kings continued to rely mainly on the customary method of the impressment of merchant ships and their crews to form fleets. Under Henry VI his father's navy was sold off or allowed to decay: as Colin Richmond has shown (1967), by the mid-1430s the crown possessed only one or two ships. A small build-up occurred under Edward IV which gained momentum from impending war with Scotland; in 1481 there were fifteen or sixteen king's ships. Henry VII had a dry dock constructed at Portsmouth; he left his son about seven ships.

The great expansion of the royal navy as a permanent force took place in Henry VIII's reign. Early in the reign dockyards were built at Woolwich and Deptford; new naval officials appeared, such as the Treasurer of the Navy and the Comptroller of the Ships, an office first mentioned in 1524, in charge of the provision and issue of materials. At his death Henry had fifty-three vessels, most of them built in the previous decade. The crown still relied on the impressment of merchant ships, but the core of its fleets now consisted of new-style warships, built to fighting specifications. The short, stubby merchant ship, broad of beam, relied for defence and attack on its raised 'castles'. Light cannon, like other missile-throwing weapons, were used on the main decks as adjuncts to large complements of soldiers whose tasks were to board the enemy and to repel boarders. But this style of armed ship was replaced by the 'gun platform' – the true warship with tiers of long interior gundecks replacing the hold, from which projected rows of heavier cannon. Enemy ships were now bombarded into submission. Nevertheless, the new warships had their captains, soldiers and crews recruited in the traditional way – by agreements with nobles to undertake captaincies and the enlistment of temporary ships' companies. The permanent royal navy remained primarily a collection of ships and stores, not men.

Did the military power of the crown increase under the

Yorkists and early Tudors? The Wars of the Roses certainly reinforced royal awareness of the need to be prepared to resist dynastic rebellions and invasions. This need was met by keeping the arraying system in efficient order and by committing royal retainers and the more reliable magnates to supply and lead contingents in emergencies. Nevertheless, Cornish rebels were able in 1497 to march right across southern England without serious challenge before they were overcome. In 1536 the king's forces under the Duke of Norfolk were too weak to challenge the Yorkshire rebels.

The Wars of the Roses, in which reliance had often been placed on foreign allies and mercenaries, kept English kings and commanders abreast of continental military developments. Henry VIII, keen to play a leading role in European affairs, fielded armies on the continent equipped with the latest artillery and with formations of pikemen and handgunners. He dispatched navies composed of new-style warships, such as the fleet which he watched at Southsea in 1545, arrayed against the French invasion force; on this occasion one of his great ships, the *Mary Rose*, sank dramatically. He had key royal fortresses modernized and a coastal defence system constructed to meet the needs of the new artillery age.

All this was enormously expensive. The costs were increased by the growing sophistication and scale of continental warfare. John Hale has pointed out (1985) that in the period 1476–1528 the size of the field armies of the major powers mostly hovered between 25,000 and 30,000, and that from 1536 to 1558 there was a sharp increase. When Henry VII invaded France in 1492 he besieged Boulogne with an army of 12,000; in 1544 his son besieged Boulogne and Montreuil with 44,000. Henry VIII was never able to match the military resources of Francis I of France or of the Emperor Charles V, and was to fall further behind them. In terms of territory gained, Henry had little to show for his efforts. In 1513 he managed to capture only Thérouanne and Tournai. In 1523 the Duke of Suffolk's promising advance along the Seine valley petered out. It was a sign of shrinking power and ambitions that the capture of Boulogne was the height of Henry's achievement in 1544.

The monarchy of the Yorkists and early Tudors was capable of fielding impressive armies and navies abroad. Its northern arrays, armed with bow and bill under the command of the Lieutenant of the Marches, the Earl of Surrey, inflicted a shattering defeat on the Scottish invasion force of James IV in

1513. These achievements were to a considerable extent built on the efficient exploitation of the traditional framework of military organization. But the crown's military capability was dwarfed by that of the Valois and Habsburg monarchies. Moreover, the crown failed to achieve a firmer military ascendancy over its subjects. In face of dynastic challenges and protest movements about 'bad government', the normal system of military obligations might prove unresponsive to the king's demands or liable in some regions to manipulation by his opponents. The vulnerability of the crown, starkly shown up by Richard III's defeat and death at Bosworth in 1485, was not cured by the early Tudors. Rebellions against Henry VII in 1486, 1487 and 1497, if they had been as well led as his own invasion force in 1485, might well have toppled him from the throne. In 1536 Henry VIII's government was saved from the Yorkshire rebels only by the restraint of Robert Aske and his fellow rebel leaders.

It was in the sphere of political symbolism that the military and naval power of the Yorkists and early Tudors had a new impressiveness, adding to the glory of kings. Gun trains, massed infantry, warships and artillery forts were the military toys and technology with which Renaissance princes sought to impress one another, and whose political effect on the courts of Europe Henry VIII in particular was determined to exploit. Some of these toys may also have helped to render rebels and their sympathizers faint-hearted. The character of the crown's military installations and hardware was becoming more clearly differentiated from those of individual subjects and communities. But though the crown claimed the monopoly of controlling military activity, its technological superiority had not yet reached a stage where the crucial contributions of nobles and communities could not be used against it.

3   Crown and Community

The Image of Royalty

In the mostly illiterate world of Yorkist and Tudor England, visual images and the spoken word were as important a means of conveying information and ideas as the written or printed page. The display in public of the person of the king, his queen, his heir and of the trappings of royalty played a key part in the creation of an impressive royal image. If the king was comely, well-built and of healthy appearance, subjects were reassured about the continuity of vigorous rule and about divine blessing on the realm. It was important that the king, when he appeared in public, rode with a martial air, displayed a gracious countenance to bystanders, and dismounted to kiss relics devoutly. This behaviour was a ritual demonstration that he valued the royal virtues of prowess, mercy and piety. When in 1471 Henry VI was led in a forlorn procession from St Paul's Cathedral through Cheapside and Cornhill, a later London chronicler commented that it 'was more like a play than the showing of a prince to win men's hearts, for by this means he lost many and won none or right few, and ever he was showed in a long blue gown of velvet as though he had no more to change with'.

The features and physique of the king were regarded as having particular importance since it was believed that physical attributes reflected spiritual qualities or defects. To promote the Lancastrian claim to the throne the story had circulated that Edmund Crouchback, Earl of Lancaster, son of Henry III and younger brother of Edward I, was in fact the elder of the sons, but that he was debarred from the throne because of his handicap. Sir Thomas More, in his *History of Richard III* written in the 1510s, vilified the king's character by denouncing his alleged physical defects: 'his limbs were ill matched and misshapen, his back hunched, one shoulder higher than the other, his face forbidding and cruel' (1986).

Conversely, reports of a king's comeliness strengthened obedience, arousing expectations that his rule would be blessed and just. An Italian in London in 1483, Dominic Mancini, reported how the promising mien of Edward V, Richard's nephew and victim, caused his disappearance to be mourned: 'He had such dignity in his whole person, and in his face such charm, that however much they might gaze he never wearied the eyes of beholders. I have seen many men burst forth into tears when mention was made of him after his removal from men's sight' (Mancini 1969).

How was such a favourable image of kingship relayed to subjects generally? Kings were frequently on the road and in the fields and woods, especially in summer. They travelled from palace to palace, visited friends in their country houses, went hunting and hawking, boarded at monastic guesthouses and worshipped at popular shrines. Henry VII and Henry VIII confined their travels much more to southern England than the Yorkist kings had done – Henry VIII went only once as far north as York. The early Tudors had fewer personal ties in the north and neglected most of their Welsh kinsfolk.

By this period there were well established and increasingly elaborate public rituals, part religious, part secular, for the 'showing' of the king, his foreign allies and his entourage to the people. These had developed in the formal receptions of kings, queens and other royal personages by citizens and burgesses. London had its customary processional route. This was followed by the Emperor Charles V and Henry VIII in 1522, when, coming from Greenwich Palace, they were met at Deptford by the citizens and escorted by them along a processional route which commenced in Southwark at London Bridge, carried on via Gracechurch Street and Cornhill to Cheapside, and ended with the monarchs entering St Paul's Cathedral for mass. At customary points along the way (for instance at the conduit in Gracechurch Street) princely processions were edified and entertained by sculpted and live tableaux contained within or associated with artificial constructions such as towers and arches spanning the street. Angelic figures hymned and censed the prince, who was greeted by personations of biblical, holy and historic figures and embodiments of allegorical ones. These made speeches or performed tableaux glorifying the prince, his dynasty, his policy, and the circumstances of the celebration.

Thus the prince entered a civic environment transformed into an extension of the heavenly one. He or she became a principal actor at successive stages of an uplifting drama. Participants and onlookers enacted the cosmic significance of princely power. Under the early Tudors, particularly Henry VIII, this sort of apotheosis of monarchy in verse and visual display became more elaborate and sophisticated in the realization of particular political themes and in their artistic and literary integration. The court painter Hans Holbein apparently collaborated with two specialists in Latin verse, John Leland and Nicholas Udall, in devising an intensely classical pageant of Mount Parnassus for the reception of Anne Boleyn as queen in London in 1533. The theme of the reception, intended to promote her popularity, was that she would secure the future of the dynasty by providing the king with a son. The propaganda value of such entries in the sixteenth century was enhanced by the printing of pamphlets containing the verses declaimed in them.

But royal entries such as these were occasional occurrences. A glorious image of royalty was projected more routinely at court, especially when king, nobles and courtiers gathered to celebrate the principal Christian holidays, and, more occasionally, royal marriages and the reception of distinguished foreign guests and envoys. In his treatise *The Governance of England*, Fortescue stoutly defended the royal practice of extravagance – the erection of new buildings 'for his [the king's] pleasure and magnificence', his purchase of rich clothes, furs and precious stones. The king ought also to buy fine furnishings for his palaces 'and horses of great price . . . and do other such noble and great costs, as suits his royal majesty' (1885). It was fitting that the king should have the most harmonious choristers available in his chapel royal, the most talented musicians in his chamber, the best falcons, hounds and pastrycooks. The crown customarily possessed the most extensive forests, warrens and fishponds; in balladry it was the king's tall deer that Robin Hood and his fellow outlaws slew. At the Tower of London the crown for centuries had had a menagerie of lions and other awesome, exotic beasts, unique in the realm, a unique symbol of majesty.

The Yorkist and early Tudor kings were able to afford a magnificent court: 'you might have seen, in those days', said one chronicler about Edward IV's reign, 'the royal court presenting no other appearance than such as fully befits a most mighty kingdom.' Remains of Edward's building works are the Great Hall at Eltham Palace (Kent), and St George's Chapel, Windsor Castle, which he commenced in the 1470s (the chapel was not completed till the 1530s). He was the first English king who willed that he should be buried in St George's, thus associating his dynasty with the international prestige of the Order of the Garter, whose chapel it was. Henry VII impressively rebuilt Sheen Palace (Surrey) on the banks of the Thames, renaming it Richmond. But this palatial housing of the monarchy was eclipsed by Henry VIII. Inheriting twelve or so houses, he left in the region of fifty at his death. From about 1535 there was a massive building programme. Most of Henry VIII's additions were to houses which he had acquired – he built from scratch only the surviving St James's Palace and the lost Nonesuch (Surrey).

Court festivities reached their climax with the 'Field of the Cloth of Gold' in 1522, when Henry met Francis I of France in the March of Calais. Henry amazed European courtly society by having a temporary, prefabricated palace, a castellated structure around a courtyard, set up near his castle of Guines. The event was staged primarily to impress other princely courts: the run of court festivities were intended to entertain select noble circles, not subjects in general. But, as we have seen, king and court were high in profile. Gossip must have permeated from court to all levels of society and throughout the realm. For it was, when fully attendant, the largest community in England, and it stayed most frequently near London, the largest centre of population. Many denizens of the court's service departments were of humble status, and so doubtless were those with whom they mingled outside it. The court was not only seen by common folk on its travels and formal entries; there were frequent occasions when some of them were admitted within its precincts, even to the king's presence. He 'touched for the evil' and his almonry daily made charitable distributions on his behalf.

Throughout the realm folk were avid for tales from court, as is illustrated by conciliar concern in periods of political tension about the spread of scurrilous rumours. But, for subjects generally, the king became most familiar through the proclamations made on his behalf, often at markets and fairs, which might order obedience to old or new statutes or more temporary measures, or might announce royal policy. In a recent article (1986) Alison Allan has shown how Edward IV's government set a new trend in the use of proclamations to justify and enforce the royal will, by systematically issuing them in English instead of Latin, and insisting that the texts be read verbatim. Consequently a precise, awesome and flattering image of Yorkist and Tudor monarchs could be projected widely, in perorations which presented them as working zealously to establish tranquillity in the realm and to correct sinful conduct within it. In a proclamation of 1526 concerning the destruction of tillage by enclosure, Henry VIII was presented as 'having tender zeal and respect above and before all other things to the honour of Almighty God, and the advancement of the commonwealth of this his realm'. He had 'in his own person travailed' concerning the matter; the 'little reformation' achieved was 'to his no little grief and displeasure' (Hughes and Larkin 1964). The man in the market-place might now receive a rounded view (however fictitious) of the royal personality, and of the king's high-minded aims, his diligence in the public cause, and his emotional commitment to reform.

Proclamations show how kings and their councillors were using the written word to a greater extent in our period to inform and manipulate public opinion. By then, though most of the populace were illiterate, a high proportion of the aristocratic and urban elites was probably to some degree literate, at least in English. The habit of reading aloud from books to instruct or entertain the less skilled or practised was well established. Annals with somewhat laboured entries recording events up to the present had for several generations been composed and circulated for London citizens. These chronicles tended to be more secular in their interests than the annals written up customarily in some monasteries; they were more consistently concerned with national affairs and more accessibly composed in English instead of Latin.

London was the centre of English book production, with booksellers clustering round the churchyard of St Paul's Cathedral. Visitors up from the country bought copies of the London chronicles, diffusing their versions of events throughout the realm. Londoners, anxious for the crown to maintain their privileges of self-government and to protect their overseas commerce, had developed a characteristic bias in favour of strong kingship, which they regarded as benefiting the realm when it benefited the city. Pro-monarchical attitudes were reflected in the London chronicles and also in the first history written by a Londoner to be printed, a work by the draper and alderman Robert Fabyan published in 1516 by the London printer Richard Pynson under the title *The New Chronicles of England and France*. The second part of this, from 1189 onwards, was in fact a London chronicle, expressing the elite's characteristic political views.

The London interpretation of English history was conveyed into the popular history-writing which developed in the sixteenth century, through works by authors such as Fabyan and Edward Hall. With little need of official encouragement English historiography became stridently pro-monarchic and pro-Tudor, a potent force in moulding views generally favourable to the role of the monarchy and in particular a widespread sense of the divine imperative of obedience.

Under the Yorkists there had been occasional officially inspired works of literary propaganda. They appear to be novel in being written in the vernacular and in the form of descriptive pamphlets. One of them, an account of the revolt against Edward IV in Lincolnshire in 1470, aimed to prove how deceitfully and treasonably its secret instigators, the Duke of Clarence and the Earl of Warwick, had behaved (Nichols 1847). The *Historie of the Arrivall in England of Edward IV* recounted his recovery of the realm in 1471, showing how God had favoured his cause (Bruce 1838). A shorter French version had been produced for circulation on the continent. Both treatises were anonymous; the writer of the *Arrivall* said that he was a servant of the king.

In 1476 the London merchant William Caxton rented a shop in the precincts of Westminster Abbey and set up there the first printing press in England. The invention and introduction of printing vastly increased the means of royal propaganda. For political purposes Yorkist and early Tudor monarchs could easily control and exploit printers in England, since there were so few of them and most of them had their businesses in London. H. S. Bennett calculated (1970) that there were about half a dozen printers at work in England *c*.1500, and about twenty *c*.1550. Censorship of printed books became a serious problem for ecclesiastical and secular authorities only in the 1520s, when Lutheran and other books condemned as heretical started to flood in from the continent. Kings employed a succession of printers (who came to style themselves in the sixteenth century as 'Printer to the King'), at first to print statutes and proclamations. A notable early example is the proclamation printed in London by William de Machlinia in 1486, a translation into English of Pope Innocent VIII's Bull giving his

44

approval to the marriage of Henry VII and Elizabeth of York, his recognition of Henry's right to the throne, and threat of excommunication to anyone who challenged the king or his heirs. As Anglo noted (1969), this key piece of propaganda was reprinted by Wynkyn de Worde in 1494 and 1495, and by Pynson in 1497.

Short texts such as this were speedily duplicated as handy broadsheets. Nailed up in a variety of public places they reached a larger potential audience than ones just read out once on a special occasion. The printed bill was a more effective source of information than its handwritten predecessor, more certainly legible and authoritative.

In the sixteenth century there developed a market for short pamphlets describing public events, which printers often catered for with accounts derived from 'official sources'. Early examples were the two pamphlets published in 1508 by the King's Printer, Richard Pynson, on the subject of the betrothal of Henry VII's daughter Mary to Prince Charles of Castile (the future Emperor Charles V). One of these was an account in Latin by the king's Latin Secretary, Pietro Carmeliano, the other a shorter English version of the same. But it was only in the 1530s that the crown started to use printed pamphlets on a large scale and (particularly under Cromwell's guidance) systematically to explain and justify royal policies. Early examples were the printing by Thomas Berthelet, King's Printer, of the opinions obtained from universities about Henry VIII's divorce process in 1530–1.

In our period the images projected of royalty were firmly and elaborately rooted in traditional beliefs and rituals. But they were much more effectively projected, and more deliberately so by royalty. This image-making was facilitated by the crown's greater wealth, by the new elaboration of pageantry, the flowering of London-based historiography and the invention of printing. By the early sixteenth century monarchs had impressive new means of imposing their views of the polity on their subjects, means which their critics found hard to match.

King and Community in Parliament

Parliaments were the occasions when the king and the 'community of the realm' formally came together and merged as one body in order to settle important matters pertaining to all. In parliaments kings appeared in front of their leading subjects and representatives of communities from most parts of the realm, seated or standing in hierarchical order as parts of a whole – the state opening of the modern British parliament is a relic of these occasions. Kings also sometimes presided over the conduct of business in the Lords.

The historians of the new monarchy were divided in opinion as to whether the constitutional position and political importance of parliament, and particularly of the Commons in parliament, increased or declined under the impact of the new monarchy. J. S. Rokwell, the historian of the medieval Commons, has argued that 'the Tudor period witnessed a contraction in parliamentary control of taxation' (1970), and that some of the medieval traditions developed in the Commons of using parliament as a means of limiting monarchical authority remained in abeyance until the seventeenth century. The main thrust of Roskell's argument is that the position of the Commons was fundamentally changed only in the late seventeenth century; it then established the basis of parliamentary control over the executive; this period, and not the Tudor one, was the time of the 'great divide' between medieval and modern parliaments. Before the 'Glorious Revolution' of 1688 the political importance of parliaments was limited by their irregularity and the control exercised by monarchs over summons. Monarchs were not obliged to summon parliaments at regular intervals or to prolong a session over a fixed term: they 'prorogued' parliaments (that is, terminated a session) and dissolved them at their pleasure.

In the century or so before the start of our period parliament had developed elaborate institutional habits and procedures. Throughout the time we are dealing with (though not always before then) parliaments were summoned to meet in the vicinity of London, at Westminster – except in 1523, when parliament met in the city, at the Dominican friary (Blackfriars). The Lords (the title House of Lords first appears in 1544) consisted of bishops, abbots and priors, sitting by virtue of their ecclesiastical offices, and secular peers (dukes, marquesses, earls, viscounts and barons), sitting by virtue of hereditary right or the creation by the king of a new peerage for an individual and his male heirs. These were all summoned by individual writ issued from Chancery. S. E. Lehmberg, the historian of the Reformation Parliament (1529 to 1536), has calculated that the holders of 107 titles sat in it (fifty ecclesiastical, fifty-seven secular) (1970). In the Commons there were seventy-four knights of the shire, two from each shire (none was elected for the franchises of Cheshire and County Durham). In 1529, 236 burgesses sat for

117 parliamentary cities and boroughs, which returned two members each, except London, which returned four.

The freeholders entitled to elect shire knights in the county court generally elected leading gentlefolk – of the status of 'knight' and 'esquire' – and the electors in the smaller boroughs tended to return non-resident gentry rather than resident merchants. Lords and Commons debated separately in the chambers assigned to them in Westminster Palace and Abbey – the Lords were housed impressively in the palace and the Commons had to make do with the abbey's chapter-house or refectory. In the king's absence the Lords were presided over by the Chancellor of the Realm. The president of the Commons was the Speaker, one of their number whom they elected at the start of their first session. The Speaker controlled the order of business and the debates in the Commons, and monopolized all formal communications on their behalf with the king and his councillors. The Commons habitually elected royal retainers to the speakership, men likely to have an understanding of royal policy and to be personally agreeable to the king.

The 'king in parliament' constituted the supreme legislative body in the realm, enacting laws (statutes) which bound all the king's subjects, overriding the common law and royal prerogative, but limited in scope over ecclesiastical matters until the statutes of 1532–4 which transferred papal authority to the king. King and Lords sat as a court, hearing important suits, such as some treason cases. The Lords were the king's council in parliament, an eminence which had not been traditionally shared by the Commons. But, as A. R. Myers pointed out (1981), the importance of their part in legislating received recognition in the formula introduced in statutes in Richard III's 1484 parliament: 'by the advice and assent of the lords spiritual and temporal and of the commons'. The Commons were seen as representing and binding the whole community. Sir John Fortescue, writing in the 1460s, had implied in *The Governance of England* how significant their rights were for the liberties of Englishmen (1885). The Commons negotiated with the crown the amount of taxation to be levied and could refuse assent to taxation; formally the Lords had a limited say over subsidies. Statutes originated in bills, some of them drafted and promoted by the king's council, which were introduced into one or other of the Houses and debated by both of them. Those that were passed (possibly in an amended form) were either refused or assented to by the king, sometimes with additional provisos tacked on.

There was no formal diminution in the constitutional role of parliament or in the privileges of the Commons in the Yorkist and early Tudor period. The crown had no settled design to undermine parliament, because kings and their councillors saw how it could be used to strengthen their power and bind subjects to obedience. Englishmen were strongly attached to parliament; an attack on its powers would have alienated them. Secular royal bureaucrats tended to share such sentiments, as well as landed aspirations, with gentlefolk in general. One leading royal servant of Henry VIII wrote that the authority of parliament in England 'is supreme and absolute'. This was Sir Thomas More, in *The History of Richard III* (More 1986). As MP for London in the 1504 parliament he had incurred Henry VII's anger by arguing successfully in the Commons for the rejection of the royal demand for taxation. But Henry punished More by devising a lawsuit against his father. The Commons did not enjoy complete freedom of speech.

Occasionally the Commons vigorously opposed Tudor financial demands, notably in 1523, when Wolsey had to accept a reduced sum after bitter opposition – though it was still an unprecedentedly huge amount. But as Roskell has pointed out (1970), the Yorkist and early Tudor Commons showed considerable docility over taxation. From Henry VII onwards monarchs were granted the right to levy customs dues for life in the first parliament of the reign. The devices developed in the fourteenth century to make grants conditional on appropriation to specific purposes fell into abeyance. As critics of royal government, the Commons were pusillanimous compared with some of their predecessors of the later fourteenth century and the Lancastrian period.

One reason may have been that gentlefolk on the whole approved of Yorkist and Tudor government, generally regarded as more competent. The king's men, now a large element in the Commons, usually inclined it towards docility. The leading royal retainers may have organised caucuses of their fellows to promote royal bills. In 1523 government pressure was put on the king's servants in the Commons in order to weaken opposition to Wolsey's tax demands. Sir John Hussey, Master of the King's Wards and Chief Butler, apparently acted as leader of the court party, stepping up the grant by the Commons. But though the government might organize a party within the Commons to get its way, there is no clear evidence that it habitually fixed elections. The large numbers of royal retainers elected probably resulted from the sheer growth in their numbers. Lehmberg has concluded that 'there is no extant proof of direct royal intervention in the elections' in 1529, though 'Henry may have asked the duke of Norfolk and some other courtiers to use their influence for him in certain areas' (1970). By 1534, Lehmberg points out, Thomas Cromwell was promoting the king's interest in by-elections to the Reformation Parliament. In 1536 the Yorkshire rebels petitioned the king's council for 'reformation for the election of knights of shire and burgesses'.

Popular confidence in the ability of parliaments to represent and defend the interests of subjects may have been on the wane. Large shortfalls in subsidies reflect widespread evasion of parliamentary taxation. Sometimes – in 1489, 1497 and 1523 – opposition took the form of demonstrations which might escalate into rebellion. The frequent summons of parliaments, according to Henry VIII's chaplain, Thomas Starkey, 'were no small trouble to the commons of this realm'. There was no protest at their infrequency – in the last five years of his reign, Edward IV summoned one parliament which lasted five weeks; in the last twelve years of his reign Henry VII summoned one parliament of nine weeks. Traditions of criticizing and amending government could not flourish as they had when there were regular parliaments, as many as one or two a year. Parliament continued to be recognized on all sides as an integral part of the constitution. Its effectiveness as a check on government had always had clear limitations; in this respect it was notably less effective in our period than in some past phases.

Crown and Magnates

Among the secular peers of parliament there were some who were distinguished by the superior hereditary titles of duke, marquess, earl and viscount. In 1523, for instance, there were two dukes, one marquess and seven earls. What the holders of such titles nearly always had in common was the possession of landed incomes which were larger than those of any other subject except some of the bishops and abbots. These lay magnates were the millionaires of their day. Land was the foundation of their wealth and political power. They wielded considerable control over the lives and fortunes of their tenants and neighbours. They expected kings to protect and foster their family interests, to entertain them regularly, to consult them about affairs of national importance and to reward them with lucrative grants and prestigious offices. In their own eyes, and those of many subjects down to the humblest, they were the 'natural' governors of society under the king, and had a special right to exercise authority in the regions where they had concentrations of estates.

In the 1460s Sir John Fortescue, formerly a judge and currently the head of the deposed Henry VI's Chancery in exile, reflected in his treatise, to be entitled *The Governance of England*, on the role of magnates in undermining Henry's rule. Fortescue argued that in England, as in other leading Christian principalities, 'overmighty' subjects had destabilized the rule of kings and sometimes usurped their thrones. Henry's dearth of disposable income had, he alleged, led to a cooling of allegiances, subjects giving more devoted service to lords who could reward them better (Fortescue 1885).

Fortescue made shrewd points about the shrinkage of the royal estates and income, which the Yorkist kings and Henry VII succeeded in reversing, and about the mushrooming growth in landed wealth and power of a handful of magnate families in the fourteenth and fifteenth centuries. There were several reasons for this aristocratic phenomenon. Frequent failures in the male line concentrated property in the hands of fewer great families. When it was feasible, nobles were concerned to pass on to their descendants an augmented or at least intact inheritance. They tried to marry their heirs to heiresses. The crown was prepared to license the use of legal devices which avoided the dispersal of an inheritance among co-heiresses or which endowed younger sons without necessarily alienating property in perpetuity. The crown provided magnates with opportunities for aggrandizement too, in war, by bestowing estates on them and by their marrying well-to-do wards. Kings elevated their kinsfolk and leading servants to magnate status by such rewards.

The local influence at the command of magnates could be of immense value to the crown. This influence was extended by the hold which they tried to secure over the loyalties and fortunes of kinsfolk, tenants and neighbours. Magnates sought to retain their services and goodwill by grants of offices, annuities, fees and favours. A 1504 statute associates with retaining: 'writing [i.e., the making of indentures], oath, promise, livery, sign, badge, token' (the last four comprising the grant either of robes in the lord's heraldic colours or of a collar or brooch in the shape of one of his emblems).

Since the fourteenth century public concern had been voiced that these forms of patronage and the public wearing of liveries facilitated corruption of the law, intimidation and riot. A royal ordinance and a statute in the last decade of the century were aimed at controlling the workings of the system. But these measures do not seem to have been effective. Magnates continued to retain widely in the fifteenth century; magnates and retainers remained prone to involve each other in their property disputes and in competition for royal office and reward. Rival caucuses caused local disturbances which might escalate and challenge royal authority. In the early 1450s there were fights in Yorkshire between the 'affinities' of the Percy family (who enjoyed court favour) and the Nevilles. This was one of the feuds which led to and prolonged the Wars of the Roses. The civil wars encouraged retaining, since rival claimants to the throne relied heavily on the ability of their leading supporters to muster men in arms.

The relatively new but long-lasting issue of the disputed right to the crown made the grievances and ambitions of 'overmighty' subjects particularly dangerous to kings in the second half of the fifteenth century. The usurpation of Henry IV in 1399 provoked recurring controversy; it provided a cause into whose sails nobles alienated from the court might blow. The matter was further unsettled by the controversial usurpations of Edward IV, Richard III and Henry VII. Since so many magnates had royal descents, the danger of attempts on the crown increased.

A traditional element in new monarchy theory has been the view that the early Tudors tackled and more or less solved the problem of the higher nobility by destroying their power – using executions and forfeitures, the curbing of retaining, and reliance on men of gentry and bourgeois origin, who rose to wealth in royal service but did not exercise the old-fashioned 'feudal' kind of noble power in the localities.

Monarchs were, indeed, highly sensitive in our period to any hint of noble plotting or even speculation about the succession. Yorkists and Tudors reacted savagely to this. Henry VII was sparing in his creation of peerage titles, and apparently attempted to control the nobility by imposing recognizances – for instance, to guarantee payment of often harsh fines or to ensure correct conduct in office. The terms of bonds were negotiated by a group of councillors, the Council Learned in the Law (among whom Edmund Dudley was prominent). At the end of the reign many peers were among the large numbers bound over, in many cases on condition of good behaviour towards an opponent. The many cancellations of recognizances early in Henry VIII's reign is a reflection of the wide sense of injustice provoked by this aspect of his father's recent rule. It was articulated by some contemporary writers and, indeed, by the penitent Dudley himself.

The crown made determined efforts by legislation to impose control on retaining and to curb the ills which stemmed from its abuses. Edward IV's 1468 statute was the forerunner of a series of early Tudor statutes which narrowly restricted the categories of men who might normally be retained. According to the 1504 statute, exception was made for those who 'by the virtue of the King's placard [warrant] or writing signed with his privy seal or signet, shall take, appoint or indent with any persons to do and be in a readiness to do the King service in war, or otherwise at his commandment.' As we have seen, early Tudor armies were partly composed of retinues raised by peers.

Alan Cameron has shown (1974) that indictments of peers and their agents, among others, for giving livery illegally or for illegal retaining were heard in the King's Bench from early in Henry VII's reign, and in conciliar courts such as that set up in 1487. He concludes that Henry 'tamed the retinue by rooting out its worst abuses and managed to adapt an institution which had proved a severe problem to his predecessors into an instrument which on the whole served its purpose well.'

The larger aim of Henry VII's policy seems to have been to discipline the magnates. But their sources of local power were not systematically destroyed in the sixteenth century by the crown; neither Henry VII nor Henry VIII set out to do so. Examples of the support these kings gave to magnate power and of their dependence on it are not hard to find. After his accession Henry VII quickly restored the Earl of Northumberland to favour, though the earl may have been disloyal in intention towards him as well as towards Richard III at Bosworth. He restored the dukedom of Buckingham to Edward Stafford, whose father had been executed by Richard, and revived the earldom of Devon for Edward Courtenay. But Thomas Howard, Earl of Surrey, who had fought stoutly for Richard against him, had to wait until Henry VIII's reign, until after he had won against the Scots at Flodden in 1513, before receiving back his father's dukedom of Norfolk.

The young Henry VIII enjoyed the companionship of leading nobles and was not averse to increasing their prestige and power; royal descent was no bar to his favour. In 1510 he granted Buckingham's brother Henry Stafford the earldom of Wiltshire and in 1514 he elevated his bosom companion Charles Brandon to Duke of Suffolk. Also in 1514 Charles Somerset (an illegitimate scion of the Beauforts) received the earldom of Worcester and in 1523 Arthur Plantagenet (an illegitimate son of Edward IV) became Viscount Lisle. In 1525 Henry raised his friend Henry Courtenay (Edward's grandson) to the marquessate of Exeter and another noble friend, Thomas Clifford, to the earldom of Cumberland. These magnates and others continued to exercise the same sort of influence as their predecessors in the localities where they had concentrations of property.

Nevertheless, in our period, a shift in the balance of power between crown and magnates – to the advantage of the former – can be discerned. This was not entirely the result of a consistent line of royal policy, but partly of a number of coincidental factors. As a result of the dynastic conflicts of the Wars of the Roses some inheritances of 'overmighty' magnates were annexed to the crown through inheritance and forfeiture. In 1461 Edward IV brought to the crown the York and March complex of inheritances. The marriages of his brothers George, Duke of Clarence, and Richard, Duke of Gloucester, to Warwick the Kingmaker's daughters was to put the great Neville inheritance into the hands of the crown. This was the result of the minority of Clarence's son Edward, Earl of Warwick, from 1478 and his forfeiture in 1499, and of Gloucester's usurpation of the crown. In 1513, however, Henry VIII restored the earldom of Salisbury to Clarence's daughter Margaret Pole. In 1521 the treason of the Duke of Buckingham brought another 'overmighty' inherit-ance into the king's hands; the Stafford family, which had a royal descent from Edward III, was never to be restored. The early Tudors did not need to develop new ducal inheritances for younger brothers and sons in the way that Edward IV had done for his disloyal brothers.

Just after our period some nobles and their family interests certainly did fall victim to a line of royal policy, but this was still not directed at the destruction of magnatial influence in general. Henry VIII's dangerous religious policies made him as suspicious of disloyalty in magnates as in other subjects, and as ruthless in striking at the suspects. The sixth earl of Northumberland (died 1537), fearful of the effects of royal disfavour and suspicion, willed his inheritance to Henry, cutting out as heir his brother, the potentially dissident Sir Thomas Percy. Magnates with royal blood, disgruntled at religious change, were swept away: the Marquess of Exeter was executed in 1539; so was Countess of Salisbury's son Lord Montague, and the aging countess herself in 1541 (her younger son Reginald Pole, the future cardinal, was one of Henry's most virulent critics from abroad).

Henry continued to rely heavily on the regional hegemonies of other magnates, such as the Earls of Cumberland, Derby and Shrewsbury and the Duke of Norfolk. But he did not always hasten to replace the hegemonies which he destroyed with those of new magnates. Direct royal influence was sometimes substituted. This continued the trends set by the absorption of estates of magnates by the crown and the expansion of its funding of patronage since 1461. By the early sixteenth century no magnate could compete with the scale of crown patronage, and no provincial court aspire to the lustre of the royal household. Moreover, the king's ability, and often readiness, to enhance the dignity of nobles (reflected in Edward IV's and Henry VIII's creations of new titles), and to reward them handsomely, gave hopes of assuring widespread loyalty and diligent service among the peerage. Loyal service to the Crown was widely coming to be seen as the justification for magnate status and power rather than the claim of hereditary right and ancient tradition.

This view was promoted in current political discourse, in which the role of nobles was regarded as one of sustaining the commonwealth by implementing the prince's commands. One of Henry VIII's Wardens of the Marches was humiliated in an unprecedented way for defaults in the conduct of his office. Guy recounts (1977) how in 1524 Wolsey appointed special commissioners to enquire into the administration of justice and to punish outrages in Yorkshire and Northumberland. Complaint was made about Lord Dacre's conduct of his Wardenships, as a result of which the Council in Star Chamber debated charges against him including 'remissness and negligence' and 'bearing [protection] of Thieves'. He submitted, confessed and was put in the Fleet prison in London. In 1525 he agreed to pay a large fine and entered into recognizances for future good behaviour.

The episode is symptomatic of the new confidence of the monarchy in handling magnates even in the remotest part of the realm. But the feudal power of the Dacres, centred on their Border barony of Gilsland in Cumberland, was to remain strong into Elizabeth's reign. The older view that noble power collapsed under the weight of the new monarchy has long been discredited. It was too sweeping an interpretation. Yet recent research suggests that the heyday of the medieval strength of the magnates was indeed passing. The balance of power was shifting towards the crown between the 1470s and 1530s, impelled by fortuitous factors, but with the Tudors sometimes adding their weight to the trend. However, both Henry VII and Henry VIII valued magnate power as an adjunct of their own and wished to be surrounded by splendid and rich nobles. Above all, they and their councillors aimed to ensure loyalty and to extract good service from the peerage. In pursuit of these aims laws were strengthened and sometimes harshly enforced, and individual nobles, some of them men who had been the king's boon companions and trusted servants, were sacrificed. Under Henry VIII some ancient local hegemonies were swept away.

The Crown and Society

When R. H. Tawney said in 1942 that the Tudors 'courted the middle classes' and argued that they showed favour to the rising commercial classes on which the new monarchy rested, he was adhering to a well-established orthodoxy (Tawney 1942). This was that a new monarchy arose which was sustained politically by an alliance between the crown and 'rising' groups in society, the gentry and bourgeoisie. Since both groups were sandwiched in status and wealth between the peerage and the mass of the common folk, and since they had an awareness of some common interests, historians felt justified in bracketing them together as 'the middle class'.

Their alliance with the crown supposedly eclipsed the ancient and dangerous power of the higher nobility, and maintained control of a potentially turbulent populace. The crown relied on the expertise of the middle class for administration, and benefited from its encouragement of their commercial enterprise through taxation. Gentry who became professional servants of the crown were enriched as landowners. More generally, the crown boosted the authority of the gentry by relying on its co-operation as members of the House of Commons (particularly in the Reformation Parliament) and in the localities as sheriffs and their deputies, justices of the peace and commissioners of various kinds. The newly powerful middle class backed vigorous, even despotic exercises of authority by the early Tudors. But in the reign of Elizabeth this alliance began to be strained, as Calvinists in and out of the Commons criticized and agitated against the queen's ecclesiastical settlement. Her critics increasingly questioned the scope of the royal prerogative. Under the early

Stuarts the consensus of crown and middle class broke down, as the middle class forged a powerful constitutional opposition in parliament.

In an essay first published in 1950, 'The Myth of the Middle Class in Tudor England', the American historian J. H. Hexter powerfully attacked the concept of the middle class which underpinned this thesis (Hexter 1961). As he pointed out, the use of the term had become so elastic as to be meaningless, including not only citizens and burgesses, but people of bourgeois and petty landed origin who through their diligence and skills rose into the ranks of the gentry or peerage. The term had come to embrace men of diverse origins with divergent careers and had come to mean simply the socially successful. Hexter proposed that the term 'middle class' should be applied solely to the bourgeoisie.

Where this group is concerned, it is hard to discern any changes in their collective wealth, status or relations with the crown and gentry in the sixteenth century (and more especially in the period under consideration) which might have enabled them to act as a new prop to monarchy. It may well be that the proportion of national wealth in the hands of merchants, burgesses and craftsmen was increasing. For instance, in the north-east of England in the later decades of the century wealth was concentrating in the hands of the Newcastle Hostmen (separately incorporated in 1600), who were monopolizing the growing coal production along the Tyne valley as well as its shipment from the Newcastle quays. There and elsewhere successful burgesses bought suburban estates and made marriage alliances with gentlefolk, thus securing 'gentle' status for their descendants. As Hexter pointed out, these were well-established paths for bourgeois social advancement. Tudor policies of confirming the monopolization of power in urban government by elites and encouraging overseas trade in the hands of monopolizing groups of merchants had precedents, too. Henry VII's former councillor Edmund Dudley (of impeccable aristocratic descent) appreciated the importance of exports, 'and specially for the wool, cloth, tin, lead, fell and hide'. But he was no friend to bourgeois pretensions. He expressed the fear that the dishonesty of English merchant exporters would ruin their trade, especially in cloth. This influential royal official placed merchants, craftsmen and artificers firmly in the ranks of the 'commonalty' (as distinct from the 'Chivalry'), alongside franklins (lesser freeholders), graziers and tillers – 'these folk may not grudge nor murmur to live in labour and pain, and the most part of their time with the sweat of their face.'

Let us consider that other supposed new prop of monarchy, the 'gentry' (a term currently in the seventeenth century). It is certainly easy to find examples of 'rising' gentry – both men who established the gentility of their family by acquiring estates through the profits of service, particularly administrative and judicial service to the crown, and men who through the same routes advanced from gentility to peerage. From the fifteenth century onwards the ranks of those following this *cursus honorum* were being swelled by successors of those who had taken a somewhat different route. Since the late eleventh century, when royal bureaucracy started its conspicuous growth, careerists in many of its leading offices had for long been clergymen, the one group who in early medieval society had notionally been *litteratus*, able to read and write in Latin, the technical language of administration as well as of religion. The aspiring civil servant of the fourteenth and fifteenth centuries sought a clergyman's education at Oxford or Cambridge and took at least minor holy orders. A notable example in our period was Thomas Wolsey, 'an honest, poor man's son', according to his biographer and servant George Cavendish. Wolsey had a university career associated particularly with Magdalen College, Oxford, making some exalted aristocratic contacts. He became chaplain in the household of Sir Richard Nanfan, King's Lieutenant at Calais, and after Nanfan's death received a chaplaincy in Henry VII's household. Wolsey's job was simply to say mass in the royal presence, but he managed to impress the king and influential royal councillors with his efficient demeanour and discreet conversation. In 1508 he performed diplomatic missions satisfactorily for Henry VII, and soon afterwards was appointed almoner to Henry VIII – the start of a meteoric rise.

By Wolsey's time the offices of the Chancery, Exchequer and Privy Seal were no longer almost entirely the preserve of 'clerks' who were in orders and celibate, as they had been in the fourteenth century. R. L. Storey, in his essay on 'Gentleman-Bureaucrats' (1982), surmises that 'the preference for lay status may . . . have first become marked among civil servants recruited in the first decade of the fifteenth century, if not slightly earlier'. 'Clergyman-bureaucrats' had sought to be rewarded mainly with grants of lucrative ecclesiastical offices (rectories, canonries, bishoprics), appointments which the king could influence or make himself in his private capacity as a property-owner.

Such ecclesiastical offices constituted permanent and largely unchanging blocs of landed interest, whose possession by celibates had little effect on the composition or wealth of the secular elites. But the 'gentleman-bureaucrats' who became predominant in the 'civil service' in the Lancastrian period wanted to found or enhance their fortunes as landed gentry. They were a new competitive element at court, petitioning for estates. Obtaining them had its effect on local politics, introducing new 'court' elements into shire society. Storey comments that in Henry VI's reign 'crown patronage was under the additional strain of having to provide for a new category of legitimate suitors, that of officials who in past times could have been rewarded by presentation to church benefices but now sought benefits appropriate to laymen' (1982).

The expansion of royal revenue under the Yorkists and Henry VII enabled the crown to solve, at least for the time being, the crisis of confidence over its capacity as a patron which had arisen for a variety of reasons in Henry VI's reign. Kings were able to distribute rewards lavishly, particularly in the form of annuities, to household officials, civil servants and the higher nobility in general. The grant of most such retaining fees carried the implied obligation that the recipients would serve the king when required in ways over and above the set duties of any royal offices which they held, for which they received wages or perquisites. Annuitants might be summoned to assemble in arms (in some cases bringing their own military retinues), or to attend on the king at court or on a royal progress. On these occasions they were expected to wear his livery – in Edward IV's case, the collar of alternate roses and sunbursts, which can still be seen in the depiction of Sir Robert Wingfield, Comptroller of his Household, in a stained-glass window in the church of East Harling in Norfolk. The Tudors favoured the Lancastrian livery collar of linked Ss.

Kings also expected their retainers to give them support in their capacity as landowners, fostering royal policy as local commissioners and in shire politics. D. A. L. Morgan has shown (1973) how Edward IV used prominent members of his household entourage, his Knights and Esquires of the Body, to help enforce his will in the localities. When he landed in Yorkshire in 1471 in order to reclaim the crown, he was joined on his southward march by knights, esquires and chaplains of his household with their individual contingents of soldiers. It is likely that the political significance of this 'king's affinity' increased by the end of the reign, since the household establishment grew. Whereas there were ten Knights of the Body in 1468, there were probably as many as thirty in 1483, and the number of esquires had increased commensurately to between thirty and forty.

Edward's successors also retained widely, with the kernel of their affinity formed by their household officers. Richard III relied especially on northern gentlefolk who, in Edward IV's reign, had looked to his patronage as the successor of the Nevilles of Raby and as King's Lieutenant in the Marches towards Scotland. The nucleus of the later Tudor court establishment is to be found partly in the future Henry VII's community of exiles at Vannes in Brittany in 1484, as R. A. Griffiths and R. S. Thomas have shown (1985).

The crown was traditionally the principal fount of reward for the medieval nobility, from dukes downwards. What was new in this period was the expansion of its role in patronizing gentlefolk, men who aspired through service to the crown to establish or enhance their families' landed status in society. As E. W. Ives has written (1987), 'developments from the middle of the fifteenth century had made the monarch the ultimate dispenser of all major employment and advancement' (a trend accelerated, Ives emphasizes, by the political developments of the 1530s). The royal court entirely eclipsed the provincial courts of magnates as centres for seeking office and reward. The 'king's affinity' not only provided him with administrative personnel for a reinvigorated central government machinery and with a core of military support – such as the retainers who fought stubbornly for Richard III at Bosworth – but a potentially more effective means of making the royal will felt and obeyed throughout the realm.

There were dangers for the monarchy in the patronage system which expanded its power. Factions, often centred on a magnate and spearheaded at court – if not by him, then by courtiers with access to the royal presence – formed and re-formed to win office and reward, and to discredit rivals. Edward IV's court and nobility were riven by faction, and so were Henry VIII's, as was to be seen most clearly in the 1530s and 1540s. Ives has pointed out how the self-indulgent Henry, sporadic in his attention to business, was vulnerable to manipulation by faction (1987). Courtiers backed by magnates and knots of powerful local interests manoeuvred to destroy ministers and favourites and to modify policies. As royal power was asserted anew under the Yorkists and early Tudors, so the pressures to exploit and control it grew.

'The king's affinity' was not a monolithic bloc which could be relied on to act in the king's interest, but a mass of competitive interests which required forceful royal control if they were to be used to the crown's advantage. Retainers who built up their local power through the king's favour could not always be relied on to put loyalty to the prince above a dynastic interest which might align them more firmly with distinctive provincial sentiments. John Hussey, a member of a well-to-do Lincolnshire family, became Esquire and then Knight of the Body to Henry VII and eventually Comptroller of his Household. In 1529 Henry VIII rewarded this distinguished retired royal servant, then well into his sixties, with a peerage. But in 1536, during the revolt of the Lincolnshire parish priests and peasants, Lord Hussey showed a lack of zeal in the king's cause, and in the following year paid the penalties of treason. So too did his contemporary, Lord Darcy, made Knight of the Garter and ennobled by Henry VIII in the year of his accession, and for long a leading military official of the king and his father on the northern borders. In 1536 Darcy yielded the strategically crucial Pontefract Castle to the Yorkshire rebels who posed a formidable threat to Henry's government. Darcy even backed the rebel cause, the Pilgrimage of Grace. 'Fye! Fye! upon the Lord Darcy, the most arrant traitor that ever lived', wrote the royal commander, Thomas Howard, Duke of Norfolk, to the king's council. Hussey and Darcy were distinguished royal servants who equivocated when they saw opportunities arising to destroy the factions at court whose domination and policies they hated.

Although the concept of an alliance between the crown and a so-called 'middle class' as a basis for the new monarchy has been shown by Hexter to be defective, we can still validly think in terms of a widening of crown patronage among the landed elites in the period, helping to swell the numbers and wealth of families with peerages and of what appears to have been an expanding gentry estate in the sixteenth century. Royal office obtained by court favour became a broader highway with more promising vistas to tempt the ambitious and talented. Consequently the crown was far better served than any other focus of power and possessed a more complex network of influence in the local elites than hitherto. But the closer relationships between 'court' and 'country' cannot be seen as a straightforward gain in power by the monarchy, allying with a rising 'middle class' of gentry. Royal patronage helped to expand and entrench secular elites which were strongly swayed by their sense of family and provincial loyalties. A corollary of this expansion and the greater intrusion of 'court' into 'country' affairs was an intensification of factious pressures at court. Shifts in relationships between the crown and social groups had diverse effects on its power and stability.

4 The New Monarchy in Theory and Practice

Royal Perceptions of the Role of the Monarchy

The recorded pronouncements by the kings of this period about the nature of their office are few. Their public attitudes are reflected in sources containing a propaganda element – the iconography of ceremonies, their proclamations, speeches and sermons by their servants and treatises written with or to gain royal approval. All these, and many other royal activities, suggest that the kings were strongly influenced, not to say hidebound, by traditional views on the exalted nature of kingship, its prerogatives and duties, and the obedience owed by subjects ranked beneath it. This traditionalism is not surprising, considering the unanimity with which the English political community clung fiercely to conservative values.

Moreover, the character of royal education in the period mostly inclined kings to sympathize with the outlook of the higher nobility. The only king among them brought up from birth as heir to the throne, Edward V, had no opportunity to rule. His father Edward IV was educated as heir to a duke until he was seventeen, the year before he ascended the throne. The opportunity for Richard III to become a king arose only when he was aged thirty-one. Henry VII had been educated as heir to an earldom and was apparently put forward as a candidate for the crown only when he was twenty-six. However, many of his formative years had been spent in France and there are indications that this gave him a detached view of English institutions and culture. Henry VIII was the one king who grew up from infancy (he was born in 1491) as the son of a reigning monarch, becoming heir apparent at the age of eleven. He was brought up in a conventional but particularly secluded way. The honour shown to him as the sole male hope of his dynasty may have inspired the exalted notion of his divinely ordained majesty displayed in his policies, in contrast to the more cautious expectations of his immediate predecessors. They grew up anticipating roles as leading peers, and were anxious when they reigned not to resume the sour life of exile which they had tasted.

The fact that the crown was seized by three nobles in the period, unexpectedly to some, and shockingly to others, gave new importance to royal propaganda. Dynasties now needed to justify their rule, and emphasized their roles as restorers of peace and power to the realm, with the blessing of divine favour. In the declaration of Edward IV's title in his first parliament in 1461, it was asserted that as a consequence of Henry IV's usurpation and murder of Richard II, England 'hath suffered the charge of intolerable persecution, punition, and tribulation'; in the 'usurper' Henry VI's reign:

> not plenty, peace, justice, good governance, policy, and virtuous conversation, but unrest, inward war and trouble, unrightwiseness, shedding and effusion of innocent blood, abusion of the laws, partiality, riot, extortion, murder, rape and vicious living, have been the guiders and leaders of the noble realm of England (Levine 1973).

The succession of Richard II's legitimate heir, Edward, had now ended this dark era. In the Act settling the crown on Richard III and his issue in 1484, it was implied that Richard's rightful rule had rescued the realm from the divine wrath – this time consequent on Edward IV's alleged adultery and vices:

> therefore no marvel that the sovereign lord and head of this land [Edward IV], being of such ungodly disposition, and provoking the ire and indignation of our Lord God, such heinous mischiefs and inconvenients . . . were used and committed in the realm among the subjects (Levine 1973).

Henry VII was the first English king who felt the need to employ an official biographer and panegyrist. In his brief Latin biography of the king, Bernard André declared that the English had wickedly repudiated Henry VI. The withdrawal of God's blessing from the realm and internecine strife had ensued. The succession of his master, Henry VII, the martyred king's rightful heir, had restored the realm's relationship with God, ensuring the blessings of tranquillity.

Henry VII attempted to emphasize and enhance the special holy status and purpose of his rule by initiating a process for the canonization of Henry VI. This king's cult as protector and miracle-worker had already spread in England under the Yorkist kings. Pilgrims visited his tomb at Chertsey Abbey in Surrey, and later at St George's Chapel, Windsor Castle (after Richard III moved his body there), to give thanks or to pray for cures. Henry VII commenced the construction of a new chapel in Westminster Abbey, which he intended as a shrine for the future royal saint, for him to lie near that of the ancient holy exemplar and protector of English kingship, St Edward the Confessor. But this pantheon of sacred monarchy was never realized. Henry VIII eventually discontinued the expensive canonization process and completed what is now known as Henry VII's Chapel as his parents' burial place.

The urgency of associating the Tudors with the posthumous reputation of Henry VI declined as their rule became more assured and better accepted. But the concept that this rule had a particular rationale and justification was not allowed to fade. It was a useful counter to Yorkist sentiment and sporadic plotting, and to speculation about the succession, prompted by the Tudors' lamentable failure to produce quiversful of sons who survived to adulthood. Papal sanction had been given to Tudor rule in the Bulls granting the dispensation for the marriage of Henry VII and Elizabeth of York in 1486. Their petition for marriage had been made, according to one of the Bulls, 'in order to end the dissensions which have prevailed between their ancestors of their respective houses or families of Lancaster and York'. The lofty, indeed holy, purpose of this union and of Tudor rule continued to be stressed in royal iconography throughout the sixteenth century. It was symbolized by the most prominently used Tudor device, the mixed rose of white and red.

Thus the Tudors proclaimed that the dynasty had a new and awesome role, elaborating on a line of propaganda developed by Edward IV and Richard III. That role was not to create a new monarchy, but to restore the shattered relationship between God and the realm, thus ensuring peace and stability. Henry VII not only emphasized his dynasty's holy fitness for the task by promoting the cult of Henry VI, he also displayed an appropriate interest in crusading, a neglected religious duty of kingship. In 1486 the king licensed the queen's uncle, Sir Edward Wydeville, to lead an English contingent on the crusade of Ferdinand and Isabella, the Catholic Kings of Spain, against the Moorish kingdom of Granada, the last Muslim foothold in Spain. Wydeville's crusading force fought with distinction at the siege of Loja. In 1492 national rejoicing at the fall of Granada was organized in England, with a celebratory mass in St Paul's Cathedral. In 1511 Henry VIII acceded to the request of his father-in-law Ferdinand of Aragon for military help against the Moors. An expedition, 1,250 strong, sailed from Plymouth to Cadiz under the command of one of Henry's most seasoned soldiers, Lord Darcy.

The king, who was often to express a desire to crusade against the Turks, took with unusual seriousness another customary royal religious duty – the combating of heresy. Henry VIII did so in a singular way for a monarch, by writing a treatise against Luther, *Assertio Septem Sacramentorum*, which was presented to Pope Leo X in 1521. A few weeks later the pope conferred on Henry the unique title of *Defensor Fidei* (Defender of the Faith). There was a great conceptual gulf between Henry's literary blast for orthodoxy, a culminating expression of the holy kingship of the early Tudors, and the enactment of the royal supremacy. Nevertheless, this arrogation may have appeared less revolutionary and incongruous in the eyes of his subjects because of the stress which his dynasty had habitually laid on its special relationship with God and the reforming mission which gave its rule a particular divine sanction.

The Yorkists and Tudors also used traditional themes to develop a secular ideology of restoration, an ideology which was later to be specifically enlisted in the propaganda campaign to justify the repudiation of papal jurisdiction, and to be used to justify extensions of royal jurisdiction. Medieval kings had insisted on their sovereign rights, their *imperium*. The Yorkists and Tudors were not the first English kings to foster respect for their sovereign status by recalling the supposed existence of an ancient British empire analogous to that of classical Rome. There was a widespread conviction that England had in early times been the centre of an 'empire' and that the imperial power its ruler could consequently claim exempted him and his dominions from the exercise of foreign jurisdiction. The concept drew its strength partly from history but mainly from pseudo-history whose mythical content was tenaciously believed to be

65

fact. According to myth, Britain had in ancient times, before the Roman conquest, been united under the sway of a line of powerful British kings, whose hegemony was reasserted after the Roman withdrawal, above all in the rule of the glorious King Arthur, who bestrode Christendom.

Since the time of Edward I (died 1307), English kings had fostered the notion that they were the heirs to Arthurian pretensions, and that the sovereign lordship which they strove to exercise over the whole of the British Isles and France derived its validity in part from Arthur's ancient British empire. Edward IV (from 1471) and Richard III were the first English kings to be depicted on their great seals wearing, when enthroned, the arched imperial crown. Yorkist and Tudor panegyrists made this imperial propaganda more personal by emphasizing the dynasties' links with the glorious British past. Genealogies of Edward IV were circulated which exhibited his descent through the Mortimer family's Welsh antecedents from the ancient British kings.

Enthusiasm for the 'British history' was stimulated by William Caxton's publication in 1484 of Sir Thomas Malory's redaction into English of the Arthurian romances, *Le Morte d'Arthur*. Two years later Henry VII had his first-born child christened Arthur. Henry's biographer André stressed his patron's descent from ancient British kings. Henry's gold sovereign issued in 1489 was the first coin to show an English king wearing the imperial crown, and the usage soon spread to lower denominations. King Arthur and other British themes often figured in Tudor civic pageantry. Part of one of the pageants which greeted the Emperor Charles V in London in 1522 consisted of a mock palace in which King Arthur, wearing the crown imperial, was seated at his Round Table, attended by princes who owed him obedience, including the kings of Wales, Scotland, Ireland, Denmark, Norway and Iceland. The association of the dynasty with King Arthur is also to be found on the ancient round table now in the Great Hall of the royal castle at Winchester, which was thought in the fifteenth century to be King Arthur's Round Table. This was painted in the early Tudor period, by the time of Charles V's visit to Winchester in 1522, with the figure of King Arthur and the seating plan of his knights – his figure and the placements radiating from a dominating central Tudor rose.

When the Yorkists and early Tudors played the British theme, it was not an entirely new performance by the English monarchy, but the impressive ways in which they orchestrated it augmented their self-confidence and prestige, and aided their extension of sovereign claims. In 1533, in the Act restraining judicial appeals to the papal court, the sovereign claim was stretched ambitiously: 'by divers sundry old authentic histories and chronicles it is manifestly declared and expressed that this realm of England is an empire.' A Tudor monarch now used this secular ideology to justify a role as the restorer of a distinct and more admirable ecclesiastical polity.

The Yorkist and early Tudor kings for the most part shared conventional views about the nature and powers of monarchy. They did not aim to break the mould, but to reconstitute what contemporaries viewed as a polity fractured by the dissensions of the fifteenth century. There was a new emphasis, in the image of royalty which they projected, on its divine sanctions and its glorious mythic origins, designed to reconcile subjects to what was in fact dynastic novelty and to inculcate the rightfulness of obedience. Since some of these royal themes were used repeatedly and with increasing elaboration, it can be assumed that they were thought to be precious and effective by kings and their councillors. In this sense their use as propaganda helped to facilitate the monarchy's boldness in breaking decisively with the ecclesiastical past in the 1530s.

Literary Views of the Yorkist and Early Tudor Monarchy

As we have seen, there was a large degree of agreement about the constitutional nature and the powers of monarchy in fifteenth-century England. The principal English historiographical school developing then projected a strongly pro-monarchical interpretation of events. New dynasties claimed to be the restorers of an ancient monarchy, not the founders of a new one. Thus it was the dynastic issue which became a focus of literary debate and controversy, rather than the issue of whether or not these dynasties had developed new institutions. This was in contrast to attitudes in France, where the Valois family was generally recognized as undoubtedly the rightful ruling family, and there was no comparable dynastic issue. Kings of France, particularly from the reigns of Charles VII (died 1461) and Louis XI (died 1483) onwards, were determined to ensure that the handful of princes who exercised various degrees of regional control should be brought more firmly under royal authority, or that their provinces should come directly under royal control. The duchy of Burgundy was seized by Louis after the death of the duke, Charles the Bold, in 1477, and the duchy of Brittany was eventually annexed to the crown, first coming under its control through the marriage of the duchess, Anne, to Charles VIII in 1489.

Pro-Valois and pro-princely writers interpreted the increase in monarchical power in opposing ways. In his histories of Charles VII and Louix XI, Thomas Basin, Bishop of Lisieux, condemned the policies of the kings as leading to tyranny. In the words of Denys Hay (1962), Basin 'is a spokesman for the forces in France which resented and resisted the slowly growing machinery of royal centralization'. On the other hand Philippe de Commynes, former councillor of Louis XI, tried to demonstrate in his *Memoirs* that the monarchy's triumph represented that of sound government over the disorderly and partisan policies of the princes. Commynes 'was, in the last resort, convinced that only a strong king could save France from internecine strife' (Hay 1962). However, in the England of the Yorkists and early Tudors there emerged no alternative view of government such as that represented by Basin.

Nevertheless, there were writers in early sixteenth-century England who recognized the strength of the monarchy – in contrast to Fortescue, who in the 1470s could only see its potential. Their criticisms were usually cautiously worded or coded and concerned the misuses, actual or to be feared, of its power. Two of these writers were, indeed, leading royal servants. Edmund Dudley (born *c*.1462) was a lawyer by profession who became a councillor of Henry VII and was one of the leading agents in implementing his harsh financial exactions in the last years of the reign. In 1509, after Henry VIII's accession, he was arrested, convicted of treason and imprisoned in the Tower of London. Before his execution in 1510, he penned in prison a short treatise, *The Tree of Commonwealth*, an example of an established genre, the treatise of advice to a ruler on government – Machiavelli's *The Prince* is another, very different, indeed unique, example of this genre. Dudley's treatise does not seem to have been influential. Only four copies survive, and it was never printed. Unlike Machiavelli, Dudley has a thoroughly conventional view of the princely role: the prince ought to be 'marciable [merciful], liberal and plenteous [bountiful]' to his subjects, 'as reason shall require. . . . Then God will reward him not only with the loving hearts of his subjects, and they to serve and obey him truly, with loving dread, which is the perfect and sure bond of all gains' (Dudley 1948).

One of the themes which Dudley develops, in a diffuse and guarded manner, is that the harsh government of Henry VII has alienated his subjects and caused the decay of the commonwealth. His criticisms are mostly in the tempered form of warnings as to how a king ought not to behave. If the king does not watch out, his subjects are likely to be oppressed by their superiors, including his servants, ostensibly acting in his interest. He ought not to 'enforce or oppress any of his subjects by imprisonment or sinister vexation, by privy Seal or letters missives, or otherwise by any of his particular counsellors, but to draw them or entreat them by due order of his laws'. He should not interfere to deny subjects due process of law, and should prevent his servants from being too zealous in their punishments – 'peradventure oftentimes the Prince shall have counsellors and servants that in his own causes will do further than conscience requireth.' If in cases touching the royal interest he is not merciful, 'it will oftentimes appear to be cruelty rather than justice – and I suppose there is no Christian king hath more need so to do than our prince and sovereign lord, considering the great number of penal Laws and statutes made in his realm for the hard and strict punishment of his subjects.' The nearest that Dudley comes to direct criticism of Henry VII is when he is arguing that royal insatiability for money loses the hearts of subjects: 'Peradventure of that appetite have there been some other of late time, and were in manner without fault, saving only that.'

Dudley was essentially a working civil servant, not a detached political thinker, and he was writing in terrifying circumstances, hardly conducive to original analysis or daring formulations. Underlying his treatise is the assumption that the monarch at the time of Henry VIII's accession had great and unbridled power. There is a warning that this could be used tyrannically, alienating subjects from the king, and an implication that Henry VII had strayed in this direction. The kind of royal abuses with which Dudley was concerned were, indeed, not new – but they do not seem to have been matters for such alarmist concern in the fifteenth century. We now know the true thoughts of the condemned Dudley about the nature of Henry VII's recent rule. J. C. Harrison discovered a plea made by him from prison, after his condemnation, to two executors of Henry to provide restitution for a long list of rich and poor individuals from whom the king had extracted fines and bonds as punishments for criminal and other offences. Dudley's concern was for the repose of his late master's soul. Many victims he described as having been 'hardly' or 'sore' dealt with, sometimes 'upon a very light ground', some enduring imprisonment as well as fines (Harrison 1972). This document is an indictment of tyranny, which Fortescue had defined thus: 'When a king ruleth his realm only to his own profit, and not to the good of his subjects' (1885).

Between 1510 and 1518 a rising lawyer in royal service composed an account of a crisis in English kingship which had occurred thirty or so years previously. Sir Thomas More's *History of Richard III*, published posthumously in 1535 – though manuscript versions circulated earlier – was to be influential. It is concerned mainly with the events of Edward IV's last years and with the usurpation by his brother Richard, Duke of Gloucester, of the throne. More wrote two differing versions simultaneously, in Latin (from which the quotations here are taken: More 1986) and in English. They both end abruptly in 1483, the first after Richard's coronation, the second just before Buckingham's rebellion against Richard in the autumn.

It is not clear why More abandoned the work – Antonia Gransden has indicated (1982) various possible reasons. One is that More's appointments in 1517 as royal councillor and Master of Requests took up his time. Another is that he may have considered that an account of Buckingham's rebellion would displease Henry and his ministers, since the duke's son, because of his royal descent and great landed wealth, was a potential threat to the Tudor dynasty. The son would certainly not have relished More's account of his father's role as Gloucester's fellow conspirator after Edward IV's death, a role motivated by his decision that 'since he could not remedy the public evil he would turn it as much as he could to his private advantage.' The current Lord Hastings would hardly have been pleased to read how his grandfather had allowed Gloucester to exploit his honourable reputation in order to entrap his opponents. Above all, though More's picture of Edward IV was on the whole favourable and contradicted the hostile one which he put into Buckingham's mouth, he may have decided it would be imprudent to publish such an eloquent denunciation of Henry VIII's grandfather (whom Henry was said to resemble physically) as a king by whom 'the entire realm was astoundingly victimised in these ways and others much like them' (More 1986). More may have realized that there was much in what he had written which was likely to offend the king and individual nobles, and that trickier subjects lay ahead which were likely to upset the Howards and the Stanleys as well as Henry.

More's *History* is often read with attention focused exclusively on the malignant figure of Richard. More was, indeed, fascinated by this anti-hero, and absorbed in reconstructing the steps by which he gained the throne. But a considerable amount of the book is taken up with the behaviour of other leading actors and of English folk in general, particularly the people of London. In various asides the *populus* is disparaged. We are told that 'the exacting of money . . . is virtually the only thing which alienates the minds of the English from a prince', and that 'the common folk . . . are easily provoked to all sorts of snap judgements.' The nobles too show a lack of good judgement: Richard, 'who had quite recently been the object of burning hatred and suspicion, gained so much love and such a reputation for honesty that he was chosen over everyone as the sole protector of the king and kingdom by the unanimous consent of the nobles.' It was the nobles' sense of outrage which Cardinal Bourchier stressed to Edward IV's widow Elizabeth Wydeville when he was misguidedly persuading her to deliver up her younger son Richard, Duke of York from sanctuary in the precincts of Westminster Abbey, to which she had fled in fear of Gloucester. The nobles are portrayed as cravenly hanging on the whims of Gloucester when he presided as Protector of the Realm at the council board.

More repeatedly levels a serious charge against nobles – and, by implication, against others connected with the royal court and administration: that they were riven by faction. It was factiousness that opened the door to Richard's usurpation, and, More implies, factiousness that leads to bad government. Richard planned to exploit 'the anger and ignorance of one faction to wipe the other out'. Edward IV had failed to resolve the divisions among his supporters, and came to fear that after his death, 'when discussion and discord polarised [them] . . . they would pay more attention to partisan interests than to stating the truth, and would often advise what was pleasant, and not what was profitable, in order to advance their own faction in the favour of the prince.' On his deathbed Edward declared that 'when everyone tries to ingratiate his own faction with the prince, the result is that his favour, more than truth and expediency, determines how people advise him.' In these circumstances the nobility becomes corrupted:

> such an odious monster is pride and lust for supremacy: and once it has crept into illustrious noblemen's hearts, it never ceases to creep forth in contentiousness until it has

> drenched all in slaughter and bloodshed, as every man
> tries first of all to be next to the greatest, then to equal
> him, and at last to excel and surpass him.

Such competitiveness, More's Edward alleged, had produced
the recent domestic strife. More singles out William Catesby as
an example of a lesser noble corrupted by this atmosphere, a
man who basely betrayed his patron Hastings in the expectation
of being rewarded with his power in Leicestershire: 'that
detestable ambition it was which originally made Catesby enlist
as a party to this execrable crime' (the plot to seize and kill
Hastings). Catesby is shown as a talented, personable lawyer, a
rising bureaucrat – an example of corruption by ambition which
More perhaps feared for himself.

More'a analysis of Richard's usurpation suggests bleakly that
the one fragile barrier against the imposition of a tyrant in
England is the probity and unity of the magnates. Richard was
able to buy or dupe them with alarming ease because they were
corrupted and blinded by faction. More did not get far enough
into Richard's reign to give a comprehensive picture of the
tyranny of his rule. His one passage reflecting on aspects of
tyranny is in Buckingham's denunciation of Edward. The duke
told the citizens of London that they were now freed from
arbitrary taxation – 'the bland, harmless-sounding "benevolence"
was used to cloak pure highway robbery'; 'immense fines were
levied for petty offences.' He claimed that individuals and their
families were ruined by unjust verdicts and false accusations on
the crown's part. As D. Kinney, the editor of the Latin text,
implies, some of Buckingham's accusations against Edward could
have been levelled with even greater force against Henry VII.

So it seems unlikely that More's interest in the Yorkist period
was merely as a fascinating subject for a literary exercise. Like
his classical exemplars, he valued history for the lessons which
it could teach. There is an underlying concern in the work about
the ease with which English monarchs might rule tyrannically,
if not restrained by a wise and virtuous nobility. The factious
competitiveness of the nobility was transparent at Henry VIII's
court; doubtless More could identify facets of his Buckingham,
Hastings and Catesby among its denizens.

In focusing attention on the roles of nobles and councillors in
relation to the ruler and the common weal (*res publica*), More
was dealing with themes which were favourites among humanists,

scholars who advocated the forms, styles and themes of classical literature and who propagated its study to provide exemplars of civic values. Humanist opinion stressed the necessity of strong government by virtuous rulers, the duty of nobles to assist them by serving in office faithfully and capably, and the duty of the generality of subjects to obey, in order to promote a godly, peaceful and prosperous commonwealth. In 1531 Sir Thomas Elyot, who had been Chief Clerk of the Council and in that year was Henry VIII's ambassador to the Emperor Charles V, published *The Book named the Governor*, dedicated to the king. People of rank, Elyot argues, most often possess the virtue necessary to govern under the prince. Elyot lays down an educational programme 'whereby they shall alway be able to serve honourably their prince, and the public weal of their country, principally if they confer all their doctrines to the most noble study of moral philosophy, which teacheth both virtues, manners, and civil policy' (1970). Elyot thus tries to imbue the nobility with the desire to study apposite literature and to strive to serve their prince and the commonweal, whose interests he tends to assume are identical. But even this ferociously loyal courtier is not entirely sycophantic in his views of monarchy. 'O what damage have ensued to princes and their realms where liberty of speech hath been restrained,' he exclaims. He insists that stability is derived from the prince's love of his people, shown in his 'affability' as well as his readiness to allow them to express their opinions. But how was one to ensure a virtuous prince? In his other works he provides the same answer as for the nobility – through the correct sort of education. The excesses of the Emperor Heliogabalus, for instance, stemmed from his 'lascivious and remiss education'.

The first general history of England written in a manner of which humanist educators could approve was published at Basel in 1534: the *Anglica Historia* written by Polydore Vergil, a cleric from Urbino in Italy who had come to England in 1502 as a papal tax collector. He received English ecclesiastical benefices and was encouraged by Henry VII to undertake his history. The first version, covering events down to 1513, survives in an autograph manuscript written in 1512–13; the first printed version, taken down to 1509, was a revision undertaken, Hay has concluded, probably between 1521 and about 1524, political prudence dictating the delay in publication (Vergil, 1950). Vergil established the fashion for dividing up English history by reigns. He concentrated on giving rounded pictures of rulers and their policies, backed by an explanatory analysis of motives and events.

As an apologist for Tudor rule, Vergil emphasizes in his *History* how Henry VII destroyed the unjust ruler, Richard III, and ended the civil wars. But he is not uncritical of the Tudors. He writes sorrowfully of the imprisonment and execution in 1499 of the 'worthy youth', the Earl of Warwick, whose only fault was his dangerous Yorkist descent; he 'had to perish in this fashion in order that there should be no surviving male heir to his family'. In his manuscript version Vergil roundly condemns the domestic policy pursued by Henry in his last years:

> he began to treat his people with more harshness and severity than had been his custom, in order (as he himself asserted) to ensure they remained more thoroughly and entirely in obedience to him ... he gradually laid aside all moderation and sank into a state of avarice. .... He began severely to punish all offenders who had committed any crime prohibited and forbidden by the laws of the realm or municipal regulations.

Vergil then turned his attention to criticizing the extortions on Henry's behalf by Richard Empson and Edmund Dudley. He clearly considered that such strictures on Henry VII and his ministers were acceptable to the young Henry VIII, providing a flattering contrast to the beneficence, widely anticipated and hailed, of his fledgling rule.

But in the printed editions of his history, Vergil cautiously moderated his criticisms of Henry VII and implied his disillusion with Henry VIII's rule in his condemnations of Wolsey, who 'with his arrogance and ambition, raised against himself the hatred of the whole people'. The king 'considered everything just and right that was suggested to him by Wolsey'; the implication is that Henry put his own interest before the common good, as his father had done. Kings, in Vergil's view – as in that of many contemporaries – were constrained only by their recognition of God's precepts embodied in natural law. Henry VII and Henry VIII flouted these by allowing their ministers to behave unjustly. Public opinion was largely ineffectual as a curb. Near the end of Henry VII's reign:

> serious men who were unwilling to tolerate this state of affairs urgently entreated the two judges [Empson and Dudley] to refrain from plotting damage for wretched

mortals and from conspiring their deaths. . . . Some
important clergymen also publicly preached their disgust
at such proceedings and at the same time exposed the
king's avarice. But these remonstrances were of no avail.
(Vergil 1950).

Equally unavailing, in Vergil's eyes, were protests against
Wolsey's government; the cardinal's fall from power in 1529
resulted solely from Henry's realization that the cardinal had
betrayed his interests in the matter of the divorce.

The writers considered so far agonized about or touched on
contemporary problems of the abuse of royal power, often in a
timid, covert manner. But one writer addressed himseslf boldly
to Henry VIII on the subject and proposed uncomfortable
solutions – his chaplain Thomas Starkey (died 1538). Between
1533 and 1536, he composed and presented to the king *A
Dialogue between Reginald Pole and Thomas Lupset* (Starkey 1948).
Pole was soon to be one of Henry's fiercest critics; Lupset had
been a lecturer in rhetoric at Oxford, and had died in 1530.
Starkey had belonged to their humanist circle. The discussion
of England's social malaise in the form of a dialogue between
them probably appealed to him not only because of its classical
precedents, but because it provided him with an excuse for
disclaiming the opinions expressed. Like Sir Thomas Elyot
(1970) Starkey believed in the necessity of reforming noble
education. But he also believed that the chief threat to politic
rule and civil order arose when 'they which have rule, corrupt
with ambition, envy or malice or any other like affect, look only
to their own singular weal, pleasure and profit', that is, practise
tyranny.

Starkey is careful to insist that Henry is a virtuous prince,
but he is equally insistent that the character of English
government and trends in English opinion on constitutional
matters facilitate tyranny. It is commonly thought, opines his
Pole, that it pertains 'to the majesty of a prince to moderate
and rule all things according to his will and pleasure; which is
without doubt and ever hath been, the greatest destruction to
this realm, yea, and to all other, that ever hath come thereto
. . . such prerogative in power granted to princes is the
destruction of all laws and policy.' Pole cites the example of
royal dispensations from the operation of statutes. Lupset
demurs, but eventually agrees that it is a great fault in the polity
that the prince may abuse his authority: 'and no restraint is
had thereof by the order of our law, but rather by law such

prerogative is given to him, insomuch that ... it is almost treason to speak anything against the same.'

Pole says that Acts of Parliament have granted the crown prerogatives which an unworthy prince could use to usurp an 'authorized tyranny': 'for the avoiding whereof here in our country the authority of the prince must be tempered and brought to order which many years by prerogatives granted thereto is grown to a manifest injury.' As a remedy, Lupset proposes the constitution of a powerfully staffed and self-perpetuating council of civil liberties to provide redress for royal abuses of the law, possessing, among other powers, authority to call parliament to resist the threat of tyranny. Not surprisingly, Starkey's incautious treatise was not published; only one copy survives.

Thus, despite the traditional and continuing strength of English opinion about the constitutional nature of English monarchy, distinguished and well-informed writers in Henry VIII's reign showed concern about recent trends in government. The problem they wrestled with was entirely different from the one which confronted Fortescue. They wished to ensure virtuous rule; its effectiveness was, they felt, less of a problem. For Vergil, the obligation on rulers to enforce God's laws was a flimsy constraint on their wills – 'we mortals, relying on our reason, are accustomed to excuse our sins to God.' A problem inherent in the nature of monarchy now loomed large in some men's eyes: the problem of tyranny.

Was There a New Monarchy?

The term 'the new monarchy' appears to have been coined by the nineteenth-century historian J. R. Green. He argued that despotic rule was introduced by Edward IV and that this undermined a more libertarian medieval constitution. The modifications of this thesis by A. J. Pollard were widely accepted. He regarded the accession of Henry VII as inaugurating a new monarchy, which he saw as a Tudor phenomenon. Pollard's new monarchy recovered the governing momentum displayed in earlier centuries by central royal institutions, but did so without destroying the medieval constitution. In the eyes of early twentieth-century historians such as Pollard, the Tudor new monarchy was significant because it was the embryonic modern state, sovereign in its claims and omnicompetent in its government. These striking changes in the crown's relationship with

76

the community were effected through the vigour and ambition of the early Tudor kings and the outstanding ability of their leading ministers. Increases in royal authority were acceptable in the community because the crown succeeded in harnessing the support of the rising 'middle class', whose loyalty to a national ideal, focused on crown and parliament, was replacing traditional feudal ties and clerical allegiances. These achievements of the new monarchy culminated in the programme of religious and political reforms largely enacted in the course of the Reformation Parliament.

More recent historians have repudiated this thesis in its various aspects. G. R. Elton has called for the rejection of the term 'the new monarchy' (1953a). Nevertheless he argued that there was a decisive advance in the ideology and institutions of the state in the 1530s. Others have had reservations both about the vital significance of institutional developments in the 1530s and of the Tudor contribution to the development of the state. Medievalists have stressed the strength of central government in earlier centuries, the continuities between Yorkist and Tudor government and the institutional achievements of Edward IV. Historians of the later Tudor and early Stuart periods have highlighted the continuing limitations of government authority, reflected, for instance, in the patchy successes in imposing religious uniformity. Government from the 1470s to the 1530s is now widely viewed as achieving the *renovation* of monarchy.

However, the term 'new monarchy' continues to be used by historians of Europe in a general and sometimes tentative way, to describe the qualitative changes which they discern in the effectiveness, power and scope of central institutions of government in many European regions in the period *c*.1450–*c*.1550, though these advances were not maintained generally in the second half of the sixteenth century. Can the term still be usefully applied to England *c*.1471–*c*.1534?

There was no new autocracy created through institutional change from either the 1470s onwards or from the 1530s, though in the 1530s the crown was to break down a good deal of historic particularism in both England and Wales and to impose government which was more national (in an anglocentric sense). Kings and councillors prior to and in our period were not striving to burst the monarchy out of a constitutional straightjacket; they agreed that the generally accepted royal prerogatives provided a sufficient basis for an authoritative conduct of government. Subjects were tenaciously attached to the view, vigorously expressed by Sir John Fortescue, that England was a 'constitutional monarchy' and were often critical and contentious about the limitations which should be placed on some exercises of the royal prerogative. But kings and councillors were not driven by the conviction that they needed to construct new autocratic defences against encroachments on their authority from the 'community of the realm'. They were usually sensitive to the community's conservatism about its collective privileges and to its attachment to traditional forms of law and administration. Monarchs prudently refrained from encroaching markedly on the workings of that 'self-government at the king's command' which had long held sway in most English shires. The control of peers and gentry over the rural administration of justice, taxation and defence remained largely intact.

When government initiated institutional change in our period, it often reinvigorated traditional offices and functions, as in the revival of the household's role as the projector of regal magnificence, and of the council's as a judicial tribunal. But some notable institutional developments were innovations or were to lead to innovations. There was the setting up of revenue agencies based on household offices, which attained a remarkable degree of financial control and effected great increases in the king's ordinary revenues. The courts of the 1530s took over some of the functions and objectives of these agencies. There was the introduction of a more effective form of subsidy, and there were moves expanding the doctrine of taxation to cover more than extraordinary expenditure. There were the appearances of an 'inner council' dominated by royal officials and concerned with policy-making, which were to culminate in the emergence of a more highly institutionalized Privy Council. There were the activities of conciliar tribunals concerned with supervising aspects of royal administration, enforcing a variety of the king's rights and of statutes and providing judicial remedies; there was the eventual emergence of the Courts of Surveyors, Wards, Star Chamber and Requests. Regional councils developed with functions akin to some exercised by the king's council – the Council of the North and the Council in the Marches of Wales, which brought the peripheries of the realm more fully under royal control.

The fifty or so years between Edward IV's recovery of the realm in 1471 and Henry VIII's declaration of Royal Supremacy in 1534 were ones in which the frequency and vigour of institutional experiment in central government are hard to parallel in any previous fifty-year period. The role of royal government had certainly been reinvigorated with lasting effect in the reigns of Henry II (1154–89) and Edward I (1272–1307), but these were bursts of reform and innovation animated by a particular king. They contrast with policies carried on and adapted by a succession of ministers and councillors for consecutive decades after 1471, aimed at the strengthening of sovereign rights and the improved provision of finance and dispensing of justice.

What was the momentum which created and sustained these bureaucratic traditions of intense activity and willingness to adapt governmental methods in our period? The unprecedentedly prolonged dynastic insecurity of the crown in the later fifteenth century gave kings and their leading servants incentives to reform. The reformist agitation over matters of finance and justice had reflected and provoked discontent particularly with the Lancastrian dynasty. Royal determination to tackle these problems decisively helped to make exercises of royal authority more acceptable. Kings worked more assiduously than many of their predecessors to influence public opinion. The crown, to enhance the king's image and broadcast his views, exploited cultural developments and technical advances – the elaboration of the masque and the royal entry, the invention of the press and the rise of the London printing trade. An unparalleled but fleeting royal domination of the contemporary media was attained.

The force of such propaganda, as well as the crown's success in meeting reformist demands, help to explain why the Commons in the parliaments of the period were relatively easily managed. The return to the Commons of large numbers of royal retainers was also helpful. Shire knights and burgesses apparently negotiated the grant of subsidies without much demur; they showed no inclination to follow precedents of attempting to control the expenditure of subsidies, or of interfering in the personnel and policies of government.

Out of parliament as well as in it the elites tended to give a more habitual and uncritical loyalty to the ruler. Magnate families ceased to provide an alternative focus for loyalties, partly as a result of accidents of inheritance, but also because the Tudors, though not 'anti-noble', were determined that magnate power should be used to sustain rather than undermine the authority of the law. There was, indeed, as a result of a variety of factors in our period, a swing in the balance of power from magnates to crown. But this was not the result of an alliance between the crown and a rising 'middle class'. In the fifteenth century there was an expanding estate of 'gentleman-bureaucrats', and the crown was better equipped to satisfy their aspirations from the 1470s onwards, completely eclipsing magnates as dispensers of patronage.

The striking institutional and political achievements of the Yorkists and Tudors in our period can be plausibly represented as revivals and renovations rather as than the establishment of a new monarchy. Moreover, the idea of a new monarchy as propounded by Green or Pollard was alien to contemporaries. Indeed, it is not surprising that kings and councillors failed to project themselves as innovators; the concept of novelty was in itself unattractive to subjects, especially in constitutional matters. Sympathy with conservative views, as well as political prudence, inclined kings to stress that their aims and achievements were essentially reconstructive, promoting the renascence of the polity. From 1461 onwards usurping kings proclaimed that they aimed to restore what they argued was a shattered relationship between God and the realm, and to end the internecine strife which had resulted from unrighteous rule.

In declaring themselves the restorers of a decayed polity, Edward IV, Richard III and Henry VII were enunciating a new role for kingship. They were arguing that the relationship of preceding kings with the community had produced disorders and instability. The view that the polity became flawed in the fifteenth century was widely accepted, as its adoption as a historical orthodoxy shows. The reforming initiatives of the new dynasties were one sort of response to the problem. Some of the methods which they tried were traditional; some were not. Bursts of institutional development altered the crown's relationship with the community, increasing its authority and facilitating the greater elaboration of sovereignty in the 1530s. In Henry VIII's reign certain commentators, some of them possessing inside knowledge of the higher workings of government, expressed misgivings about the concentration of power in the king's hands and about some of the ways in which it had recently been exercised. Such sentiments were absent from fifteenth-century commentaries, except when they were blatantly propagandist. These Henrician writers sensed the rise of more authoritarian rule and feared that the dangers of tyranny, with which they were familiar from classical texts, had arisen in England.

The use of the expression 'the new monarchy' has been allowed to drop too readily from the historian's vocabulary. It is still a meaningful way of describing the Yorkist and early Tudor regimes when understood in a different sense from that of Green or Pollard. The monarchy of our period was essentially the medieval monarchy, and in some respects was to remain so at least until the Civil War. In the 1530s the crown made claims and arrogated to itself powers which were to be important in promoting the ideals and mechanisms of the modern state, but that was to be a long-term evolution. The powers of taxation, the control of military resources, and the influence in provincial affairs exercised by Elizabeth and the early Stuarts were in notable respects markedly more impressive or effective than Edward IV's in 1471 – but they were still limited. What, essentially, was new about the new monarchy is more intangible; it is the sense of mission found in the statements by Edward IV and his successors about the divine purpose animating their rule, and in Wolsey's zeal for the enforcement of justice. In brief, what had changed was the motivation of kings and ministers.

References and Guide to
Further Reading

An asterisk denotes books particularly relevant for further reading.

Allan, A. 1986: Royal propaganda and the proclamations of Edward IV. *Bulletin of the Institute of Historical Research*, 59, 146–54.

Alsop, J. D. 1982: The theory and practice of Tudor taxation. *English Historical Review*, 97, 1–30.

*Alsop, J. D. 1986: The structure of early Tudor finance, *c.*1509–1558. In C. Coleman and D. Starkey (eds), *Revolution Reassessed*, Oxford: Clarendon Press, 135–62.

*Anglo, S. 1969: *Spectacle Pageantry and Early Tudor Policy*. Oxford: Oxford Univ. Press.

Baumer, F. Le Van 1940: *The Early Tudor Theory of Kingship*. New Haven: Yale Univ. Press.

Beckingsale, B. W. 1969: The characteristics of the Tudor north. *Northern History*, 4, 1969, 67–83.

Bennett, H. S. 1970: *English Books and Readers 1475 to 1557*. Cambridge: Cambridge Univ. Press.

*Brooks, F. W. 1966: *The Council of the North*. London: Historical Association.

Brown, A. L. 1969: The king's councillors in fifteenth-century England. *Transactions of the Royal Historical Society*, 5th series, 19, 95–118.

Bruce, J. (ed.) 1838: *Historie of the Arrivall of King Edward IV, A.D.1471*. London: Camden Society.

Bush, M. L. 1970: The Tudors and the royal race. *History*, 55, 37–48.

Cameron, A. 1974: The giving of livery and retaining in Henry VII's reign. *Renaissance and Modern Studies*, 18, 17–35.

*Chrimes, S. B. 1936: *English Constitutional Ideas in the Fifteenth Century*. Cambridge: Cambridge Univ. Press.

*Chrimes, S. B. 1972: *Henry VII*. London: Eyre Methuen.

Cruickshank, C. G. 1969: *Army Royal. Henry VIII's Invasion of France,*

1513. Oxford: Oxford Univ. Press.

*Dudley, Edmund 1948: *The Tree of Commonwealth*, ed. D. M. Brodie. Cambridge: Cambridge Univ. Press.

Elliott, J. H. 1963: *Imperial Spain 1469–1716*. London: Edward Arnold.

Elton, G. R. 1953a: Book review in *English Historical Review*, 68, 276–80.

*Elton, G. R. 1953b: *The Tudor Revolution in Government*. Cambridge: Cambridge Univ. Press.

*Elton, G. R. 1971: *England under the Tudors*. London: Methuen.

*Elton, G. R. 1972: *Policy and Police. Enforcement of the Reformation in the Age of Thomas Cromwell*. Cambridge: Cambridge Univ. Press.

*Elton, G. R. 1973: *Reform and Renewal. Thomas Cromwell and the Common Weal*. Cambridge: Cambridge Univ. Press.

*Elton, G. R. 1974: *Henry VIII*. London: Historical Association.

*Elton, G. R. (ed.) 1982: *The Tudor Constitution*. Cambridge: Cambridge Univ. Press.

*Elyot, Sir Thomas 1970: *The Book Named the Governor*, ed. S. E. Lehmberg. London: Dent (Everyman's Library).

*Fletcher, A. 1968: *Tudor Rebellions*. London: Longman.

*Fortescue, Sir John 1885: *The Governance of England*, ed. C. Plummer. Oxford: Oxford Univ. Press.

*Fortescue, Sir John 1949: *De Laudibus Legum Angliae*, ed. and trans. S. B. Chrimes. Cambridge: Cambridge Univ. Press.

Gransden, A. 1982: *Historical Writing in England* vol. ii. Ithaca, NY: Cornell Univ. Press.

Grant, A. 1985: *Henry VII*. London: Methuen.

*Graves, M. A. R. 1985: *The Tudor Parliaments. Crown, Lords and Commons 1485–1603*. London and New York: Longman.

Green, J. R. 1893: *A Short History of the English People*, vol. ii. London: Macmillan.

Griffiths, R. A. and Thomas, R. S. 1985: *The Making of the Tudor Dynasty*. Gloucester: Allan Sutton.

Guy, J. A. 1975: The Early-Tudor Star Chamber. In D. Jenkins (ed.), *Legal History Studies 1972*, Cardiff: Univ. of Wales Press, 122–28.

*Guy, J. A. 1977: *The Cardinal's Court*. Totowa, NJ: Rowman and Littlefield.

*Guy, J. A. 1986: The Privy Council: revolution or evolution. In C. Coleman and D. Starkey (eds), *Revolution Reassessed*, Oxford: Clarendon Press, 59–86.

*Hale, J. R. 1985: *War and Society in Renaissance Europe 1450–1620*. London: Fontana.

Harrison, C. J. 1972: The petition of Edmund Dudley. *English Historical Review*, 87, 82–99.

Harriss, G. L. 1963: A revolution in Tudor history? Medieval government and statecraft. *Past and Present*, 25, 8–38.

Hay, D. 1962: History and historians in France and England during the fifteenth century. *Bulletin of the Institute of Historical Research*, 35, 111–27.

*Hexter, J. H. 1961: The education of the aristocracy in the Renaissance. In his *Reappraisals in History*. London: Longman, 45–70.

*Hexter, J. H. 1961: The myth of the middle class in Tudor England. In his *Reappraisals in History*, London: Longman, 71–116.

Hughes, P. L. and Larkin, J. F. (eds) 1964: *Tudor Royal Proclamatións*, vol. i. New Haven: Yale Univ. Press.

*Ives, E.W. 1987: *Faction in Tudor England*. London: Historical Association (New Appreciations in History).

*James, M. 1966: *A Tudor Magnate and the Tudor State: Henry Fifth Earl of Northumberland*. York: Univ. of York (Borthwick Papers, no. 30).

Kipling, G. 1977: *The Triumph of Honour*. Leiden: Sir Thomas Browne Institute.

Koenigsberger, H. G. 1971: *Estates and Revolutions. Essays in Early Modern European History*. Ithaca and London: Cornell Univ. Press.

Lander, J. R. 1976: *Crown and Nobility, 1450–1509*. London: Edward Arnold.

Lander, J. R. 1977: *Conflict and Stability in Fifteenth-Century England*. London: Hutchinson.

*Lander, J. R. 1980: *Government and Community: England 1450–1509*. London: Edward Arnold.

Lehmberg, S. E. 1961: Star Chamber: 1485–1509. *The Huntington Library Quarterly*, 24, 189–214.

*Lehmberg, S. E. 1970: *The Reformation Parliament 1529–1536*. Cambridge: Cambridge Univ. Press.

*Levine, M. 1973: *Tudor Dynastic Problems 1460–1571*. London: Allen and Unwin.

*Loades, D. 1986: *The Tudor Court*. London: Batsford.

*Machiavelli, Niccolò 1961: *The Prince*, ed. G. Bull. Harmondsworth: Penguin.

Mackie, J. D. 1952: *The Earlier Tudors 1485–1558*. In the Oxford History of England. Oxford: Clarendon Press.

Mancini, Dominic 1969: *The Usurpation of Richard III*, ed. G. A. J. Armstrong. Oxford: Clarendon Press.

*More, Sir Thomas 1986: *The History of Richard III*. In D. Kinney (ed.), *The Complete Works of Sir Thomas More*, vol. xv, New Haven: Yale Univ. Press.

Morgan, D. A. L. 1973: The king's affinity in the polity of Yorkist England. *Transactions of the Royal Historical Society*, 5th series, 23, 1–26.

*Myers, A. R. 1959: *The Household of Edward IV*. Manchester: Manchester Univ. Press.

*Myers, A. R. 1981: Parliament, 1422–1509. In R. G. Davies and J. H. Denton (eds), *The English Parliament in the Middle Ages*, Manchester: Manchester Univ. Press, 141–84.

Nichols, J. G. (ed.) 1847: Chronicle of the Rebellion in Lincolnshire, 1470. In *Camden Miscellany*. London: Camden Society.

Pickthorn, K. 1934a: *Early Tudor Government: Henry VII*. Cambridge: Cambridge Univ. Press.

Pickthorn, K. 1934b: *Early Tudor Government: Henry VIII*. Cambridge: Cambridge Univ. Press.

*Pollard, A. F. 1910: The New Monarchy. In *Factors in Modern History*, London: Constable, 52–78.

Richmond, C. F. 1967: English naval power in the fifteenth century. *History*, 52, 1–15.

*Roskell, J. S. 1970: Perspectives in English Parliamentary History. In E. B. Fryde and E. Miller (eds), *Historical Studies of the English Parliament*, vol. ii, Cambridge: Cambridge Univ. Press, 296–323.

*Ross, C. 1974: *Edward IV*. London: Eyre Methuen.

*Ross, C. 1981: *Richard III*. London: Eyre Methuen.

Russell, J. G. 1969: *The Field of the Cloth of Gold*. London: Routledge.

*Scarisbrick, J. J. 1968: *Henry VIII*. London: Eyre and Spottiswoode.

Shennan, J. H. 1974: *The Origins of the Modern European State*. London: Hutchinson.

*Starkey, D. 1986a: Court and Government. In C. Coleman and D. Starkey (eds), *Revolution Reassessed*, Oxford: Clarendon Press, 29–58.

*Starkey, D. 1986b: After the Revolution. In C. Coleman and D. Starkey (eds), *Revolution Reassessed*, Oxford: Clarendon Press, 199–208.

*Starkey, Thomas 1948: *A Dialogue between Reginald Pole and Thomas Lupset*, ed. K. M. Burton. London: Chatto and Windus.

Storey, R. L. 1982: Gentleman-bureaucrats. In C. H. Clough (ed.), *Profession, Vocation and Culture in Later Medieval England*. Liverpool: Liverpool Univ. Press, 90–129.

*Strong, R. 1973: *Splendour at Court*. London: Weidenfeld and Nicolson.

Tawney, R. H. 1942: *Harrington's Interpretation of his Age*. London: British Academy.

*Vergil, Polydore, 1950: *The Anglica Historia . . . 1485–1537*, ed. D. Hay. London: Royal Historical Society (Camden series, lxxiv).

Virgoe, R. 1978: The recovery of the Howards in East Anglia, 1485 to 1529. In E. W. Ives, R. J. Knecht and J. J. Scarisbrick (eds), *Wealth and Power in Tudor England*, London: The Athlone Press, 1–20.

Williams, Penry 1963: A revolution in Tudor history? The Tudor state. *Past and Present*, 25, 39–58.

*Williams, Penry 1979: *The Tudor Regime*. Oxford: Oxford Univ. Press.

*Wolffe, B. P. 1970: *The Crown Lands 1461–1536*. London: Allen and Unwin.

Wolffe, B. P. 1971: *The Royal Demesne in English History*. London: Allen and Unwin.

Index